The Story Of…

SHIRLEY B. NOVACK

Fulton Books, Inc.
Meadville, PA

Published by Fulton Books 2021

ISBN 978-1-63860-731-1 (paperback)
ISBN 978-1-63860-733-5 (hardcover)
ISBN 978-1-63860-732-8 (digital)

Printed in the United States of America

For my father, Samuel Kaufman

Prologue

"Hello, my landsman."

It was a brief sentence, but it made the hair on the back of Jacob's neck stand straight up.

"I understand you are the best artisan in the city."

The voice was unmistakable. It was a voice with a certain inflection that Jacob would never forget. It brought back a memory that Jacob had shoved in the recesses of his mind and now was forced to remember. It was gravelly and menacing, even though this was not a menacing situation.

Jacob could feel his heart rate soar. Sweat permeated his temples. As Jacob slowly turned around to face this patron, he realized that he had never before seen the man's face but he remembered a discerning physical defect.

Now there was no denying who this person was. Many years and thousands of miles had passed, yet their paths were about to cross again.

Chapter 1

Jacob

December 10, 1904, was, by all accounts, an uneventful day but for the birth of Jacob Kalinsky. Born to Sarah and Max, he was their first-born. Max was a poor chicken farmer in the town of Koretz, Poland. Sarah was his buxom wife, who was a kind, nurturing woman.

The same could not be said of Max. He was sullen and quick to anger. It was believed by most that he was born that way. Sarah always thought that bringing a child into their lives would soften him. Unfortunately, that was not the case. Max never looked at Jacob with loving eyes but more as another mouth to feed—at least until Jacob was old enough to help with chores and earn his keep.

Three years later, Sarah would give birth again. After a long and difficult labor, Heschel was born. Jacob was so happy to have this small brother to share days with. The idea of an additional son did nothing to calm the anger in Max. Although he would ultimately have another set of hands to help with the farm, it was yet another mouth to feed.

Sarah, on the other hand, compensated for Max's roughness by giving her boys all the sweetness and love a mother should have for her children. Max, after all, treated her no better than he did anyone else. It was the beginning of the twentieth century, and women had a certain place in the home as a wife and mother. Sarah knew this and never expected any more than what she had. Her boys were her life. Max was her tolerance.

Eventually, life followed a certain pattern. As Jacob got older, he was given more responsibilities. He cared for the chickens, cleaned their stalls, and milked the cows, and by the time evening rolled around, he barely made it into his bed and would fall asleep. There was a rhythm to this, and he did not know of any other life. Playing outside with other boys in the village was not routine in his world.

The only time Max would deviate from allowing his boys to have any solace was on Friday evenings. Jacob would bathe and look forward to the Shabbos meal Sarah would prepare. He loved the solemnness of her bending over the Shabbos candles as she welcomed in the Sabbath. This would be followed by a hearty meal of soup and chicken.

As Heschel got older, he joined Jacob in all the rituals afforded them. This included all the heavy chores that were really not meant for children. Heschel also loved his Friday nights and adored Sarah.

Sarah relished the time spent with her sons. Although Max was a man who rarely had any kind of meaningful conversation, she found happiness when she could be with her boys. She hated the way Max treated them with so much indifference.

Sarah was a kindhearted soul who could find a semblance of happiness in almost anything. Hard as she tried, she could not find any happiness with Max, but the times dictated how you spent your life and with whom you were to spend your life.

Chapter 2

Sarah

Sarah's family was not prosperous. Being that there was hardly any dowry to speak of, her arranged marriage would have to be with a man of similar background. She could only hope for a kind man who would not be too old or scruffy.

When the day finally arrived that she was to meet the man she would spend the rest of her life with, she could barely breathe. The only kind thing that she feared was that he not be too old nor too large or ugly.

Max, however, did nothing to hide his disdain for women or children. He was gruff, and even though he surely bathed for his wedding day, he was unkempt and made no effort to be at all soft.

Sarah could not believe that her father had arranged a marriage with such an unkind person. Her father assured her that in time, Max would come around and love could be learned.

She would follow in the footsteps of other women of this time and become a good wife to Max. The question was, would he be a good husband to her?

It was not unusual in that time to meet one's husband after one reached the chuppah. More often than not, the bride and groom were total strangers on their wedding day. Often, the groom was just as shy as the bride, and kindness and understanding would prevail. This was not the case with Max.

Max barely made an attempt to look at Sarah or get to know her. His only concern was to bring his "bride" home to learn the ways of his farm and cook a hearty meal.

Finally, the vows were spoken, the wine and challah consumed, and Sarah had to leave her family, get in Max's carriage, and head for his home. Being alone with Max scared her to death. She had never been alone with a man before, and certainly, there was no understanding on Max's part to take it slow and be gentle. He was barely acknowledging her. Sarah had never felt so alone in her life.

That night, Max made no effort to be gentle. He took Sarah to his bed as if she was a new possession and made her understand what her wifely duties were.

How, she thought, could her father promise her to this miserable man? If this was what a woman's destiny was, she wanted no part of it but had no choice in the matter.

She relished the mornings when Max would leave the house to tend to the barn and leave her to her household chores. The first ray of sunshine came when Sarah realized that she was with child. Being a mother would be a great diversion from Max, and she could pour all the love she had onto her child. She made up her mind then and there that she would become strong enough to protect her child from Max's meanness. Perhaps, she thought, the child would soften Max somewhat.

It was unfortunate that this never happened. When the baby finally came into this world, Sarah immediately fell in love with him and created a protective world around him. She decided to name him Jacob. Max had little interest in being a father and had no interest at all in what she named the child.

When Jacob was two years old, Sarah found herself once again carrying a baby. At least she knew that for the duration of her pregnancy, Max would not make any advances toward her. He barely acknowledged her existence to begin with, which, in fact, actually made life more bearable.

Finally, just short of Jacob's third birthday, Heschel was born. Jacob was so excited to have a baby brother. Sarah was filled with joy at having another baby to care for. Max remained sullen. All he thought of was having another mouth to feed until Heschel was old enough to help with the chores.

By the time Jacob was eleven and Heschel eight years of age, Sarah began to show signs of exhaustion. No one spoke of it, but Jacob became frightened at the dark circles shadowing Sarah's eyes. He would often find her staring out at the pasture in deep thought. This was not typical of her, and being a keen observer, he could not help but be concerned. Even at his young age, he knew something was not quite right.

As time went on, Sarah became more and more weak. Eventually, Max forbade the boys to see her at all. Neither Jacob nor Heschel ever had the chance to say goodbye to their beloved mother.

Chapter 3

A New Reality

It was unusually hot for a fall afternoon, yet Jacob was chilled to the bone. He could not help but shiver as he watched the simple pine box being lowered into the ground. Although he was only twelve years old, he felt a hundred.

"Jacob," his brother whispered. "Where is Mama? Why are we here?"

Heschel held on to Jacob's hand tightly as dirt was shoveled over the box in the ground. How does one tell a nine-year-old child that his mother is gone, that she is in the box and he will never see her again? How does one explain that the gruff-looking man, who looked more angry than grief-stricken, was now their only family?

"Mama is with God now, Heschel."

It had been weeks since they were allowed to see or talk to their sick mother. No one spoke of her illness, but it was made clear that children's noise would only make her suffer more. The not knowing was torture.

"Certainly," they discussed, "Mama would feel so much better if she knew we were with her."

Papa would shoo them away any time they tried to sneak into her room.

"Children are to be seen and not heard from!" he would shout.

"Go outside and tend to the chickens!" he would roar.

Now he was their only family, and the only comfort they would have would be from each other.

Somehow or other, Jacob and Heschel stayed out of Max's way so as not to receive his wrath. He was a mean-tempered man who reflected none of the love a father should have for his children.

One night a week, Max would disappear for hours without saying a word. Jacob relished the peace he would have on these evenings. It was 1916 Koretz, Poland, and stories of uprisings and pogroms were all around. Every now and then, they would hear stories from people in the village of a great land called America. The stories of villages being ransacked and burned were all around them. No one felt safe anymore.

Three months after Sarah's death, Max approached the boys with a plan. "I am going to America to start a new life. When I have enough money, I will send for you."

"But what of us?" asked Jacob. "Who will care for us?"

Max explained that he had made provisions to place the boys in the care of a friend of his. "A very nice woman," he said, "who owns a large house with many other women living there."

At twelve years old, Jacob could not fathom who this was or why anyone would take care of two young boys they did not know. Furthermore, the thought crossed Jacob's mind that he and Heschel would be the only males in the home.

"For your keep," said Max, "you will tend to her chores. Milk cows, clean, scrub floors, and do everyone's bidding. You will not complain."

The next day, the boys placed whatever scant belongings they had into pillow covers and were brought to Jordanna's home. Sarah had never been missed more by Jacob than the moment he arrived. It was a long journey by foot, and Max was too quick to bid the boys goodbye with a promise of sending for them soon.

As they were led into the drawing room, both their mouths fell open at the sight before them. Several scantily dressed women were draped over opulent sofas.

There was a divan in the corner that caught Jacob's eye. The young girl sitting on this particular piece of furniture had a sad, faraway look about her. Being so young and inexperienced, Jacob could not put his finger on it, but something about the look on her face drew him to her.

He had also never before seen a piece of furniture like this one. It had a wood frame and curved around much higher on one side than the other. Although it was large enough to lie down on, the girl was crouched tightly in a corner. It was as if she was trying to become invisible in the fabric.

The room itself was large, inviting, and lavish. Jacob had never seen anything like it before. The thought that they would now be living here both surprised and amused Jacob. Heschel just held on to him tighter. They were poor village farmers who had never been subjected to this kind of opulence.

A sweet melodic voice came up behind him.

"You boys must be hungry. Let's get you settled and find you something to eat. I am Jordanna, and this is my home."

Chapter 4

Jordanna

The last birthday Jordanna remembered having was her twelfth. She developed rapidly and could easily pass for fifteen or sixteen years of age. It was with this thought in mind that her father would tell her over and over that she really was older than she thought, than she knew.

The people in the village she lived in were either poor or poorer. Jordanna was the oldest of seven children, and food and milk was scarce. The soldiers would come into town and offer her father money for an opportunity to take his beautiful child/daughter/woman into the barn.

At first, Jordanna's father would push these men away and protect his daughter from their advances. Little by little, food became scarcer, so it was out of extreme desperation that Joel, Jordanna's father, acquiesced and handed his beautiful daughter over to a young soldier. He would explain later that Jordanna was actually a hero and that she was saving her family's life by allowing this man to do his bidding. He had many mouths to feed, and these were tough times that called for tough decisions.

She had no choice but to obey. The young soldier became two young soldiers and then three.

At first, Joel would walk away so he wouldn't hear her cries for help. Eventually, Jordanna just escaped the reality of this horrible situation. She was, after all, saving her family. At twelve years old, she was no longer a child.

It was through this experience that Jordanna learned the art of survival. As soon as she could, she ran away and ended up in Koretz, a small village in Poland. She made a living doing chores for the shopkeepers in the village. Anything was better than what she had endured.

She left home and never looked back. She often thought of how a father could do what he did to his daughter. She felt neither guilt nor remorse for leaving. She was now fifteen years old and had suffered for more than two years before getting the courage to run.

One of the shopkeepers, the butcher, was a very kind man whose wife had recently passed away. He desperately needed someone to run the home and care for his two young children. Jordanna trusted this man and felt safe there. She loved the children and eventually moved in and cared for the butcher's children and home.

As time went on, Chaim, the butcher, recognized that Jordanna had a kind but fractured heart. She never spoke of where she came from or how she ended up in Koretz. She never spoke of her family or of the horrible things she had endured. She was also quite beautiful but hiding behind a sadness that would sometimes come through. By now, Jordanna was perhaps seventeen or eighteen years old. She had lost track of what her real age was.

One night, Chaim came to her with a proposition. Although he was a man many years her senior, he would marry her and take care of her the rest of her life. His children cared for her, and it was only natural that he should remarry. She would never go hungry. In time, hopefully, she would learn to love him, and they could live a fine but humble life together.

This was, by far, the most kindness that Jordanna had ever experienced. In time, she accepted his proposal. He was a bit overweight, a bit old, and a bit weathered, but he treated Jordanna with more respect than anyone ever had in her entire life. Although she was not in love with him, she gave him back the respect he deserved and cared for what was now their home and their children. She gave to Chaim whatever she had left in her spirit, and though she hated any intimacy they might have, it was never as bad as what she had endured before.

Three years had passed, and Jordanna fell into a comfortable but never completely happy life. She had not yet found herself with child and attributed this to damage from her younger years. She loved Chaim's children like her own and felt fulfilled. She never fell "in love" with Chaim but did love him as a person, and he was always thoughtful and kind to her. Life may not have been perfect but was still much better than most—up until that fateful day.

Chaim had been promising the children that when the circus came into a neighboring town, he would take them. The joy they felt on this particular day brought tears to Chaim's eyes. They were little more than babies when they lost their mother and to have found Jordanna, who was wonderful to them, and to be able to give them this wonderful day was overwhelming.

Jordanna dressed the girls in brightly covered smocks and painted their faces. They were the happiest she had ever seen them. In fact, even Jordanna's heart swelled with pride. These were, in fact, *her* children, and she loved them with a mother's love.

Chaim packed his two children into the wagon, and Jordanna could hear the squeals of delight coming from the carriage. Even though she opted out of this outing, she watched her family head out to the next town, where the big tent had been put up. It was a two-hour ride, and Chaim wanted to get an early start. This gave Jordanna a precious day for herself, so she opted to stay at home rather than join them. Her plan was to prepare a feast for their return and listen to all the adventures they will have experienced.

By nightfall, they still had not returned.

What possibly could have happened?

It was not much later that a knock on her door realized her worst fears. It seemed the entire village had come.

What, she thought, *could have happened?*

Reluctantly, one of the villagers sat her down and gave her the news. Softly, Rhea, the village elder, spoke.

"Jordanna," she began, "there has been a terrible accident. A stampede, which began when a lion got loose, resulted in several elephants going wild. There was pandemonium, with people trampling each other and animals running in every direction. No one was safe."

Rhea could barely look at Jordanna's eyes, which by now had welled up with tears.

"It seemed to take forever for the dust to settle, but when it did, two lions and one tiger were still missing. All the other animals were accounted for." Rhea did not have the heart to go on.

Jordanna knew by now that the worst had happened, and she was inconsolable. The news the next day let everyone know that the tent had collapsed and twenty-seven people were dead. Among them were Chaim and his children.

The silence was deafening. Her family was gone, and Jordanna was once again alone.

The women in town rallied to her side and gave all the support they could, but no one could understand the depth of her despair. No one knew the hardships she had already endured in her young life. To now lose any and all sense of security and future was more than she could deal with. She could not and would not go back to her family. She left that behind long ago.

At least she still had a roof over her head and would find a way to get along without Chaim and the children. She had grown to love the children and treated them as her own. The loss created an emptiness that was too much to bear. Chaim always made her feel that he would be there to take care of her, and now she was alone.

Jordanna took to bed for weeks. The women in town would check on her daily and bring her food, but she never ventured out. At night, the streets were filled with soldiers and women selling themselves as her father had once sold her.

One night, Jordanna left her home and wandered the streets. She came upon a young girl who was new to this world and was fighting off the advances of a Bolshevik soldier. Not caring what could happen to herself, she lunged at the soldier, screaming, "Get away from her!"

The soldier slapped her down, saying, "There are enough women available. I do not need to put up with this." He left.

Surprised, the young girl helped Jordanna up. "Thank you. I thought I could go through with this, and if you had not come along, I don't know what would have happened."

Two sad souls forming a kinship through grief.

"Come," said Jordanna. "My home is not far, and I will take you there."

Once home, Jordanna learned that the girl was sixteen years old and had been thrown out of her home by her abusive stepfather. She knew of no way to take care of herself and had put herself on the street out of desperation. There was no protection from abusive men, no protection from the cold, no guarantee of food.

It was then that Jordanna came up with an idea that would someday in the future help mold Jacob's and Heschel's lives.

Chapter 5

The Brothel

The home was large and comfortable. It did not take long for Jordanna to approach the women on the streets and offer them housing and food. If they were selling themselves on the street, they could do it in a much-more controlled environment and have protection at the same time, along with a roof over their heads. In return, Jordanna would make a living and not be alone. She would also control who could come in and who could not. Jordanna would oversee everything and partake of nothing.

Her brothel became a haven for many men. Among them was Max, the poor chicken farmer from the nearby village. Once a week, Max would clean up and head to Jordanna's. He was a widower with two young sons. He was gruff, and he was nasty; but Jordanna had a way to tame him and soften him as much as possible. She would always set Max up with a girl who could make him forget his real existence.

Once a week, like clockwork, Max would make himself somewhat presentable, leave his sons, and go to town. His sons never knew where he was going or why, but they relished the times he would leave, so they did not ask.

When Max announced that he was leaving for America and was planning to leave the boys with Jordanna, they had no idea where they were going or with whom they would be staying. Max trusted Jordanna to watch over his sons and promised to send money whenever possible. In return, Jacob and Heschel would do whatever chores Jordanna required of them.

Never could they have imagined the education they would be receiving at the same time. The boys had never been exposed to much in their lifetime. All they had ever known was the farm, a mother who was now gone, a mean-tempered father, and very hard work.

Chapter 6

Becoming a Man

The first morning at Jordanna's, Jacob awoke with a start. He had never slept in such a warm and comfortable bed.

After he and Heschel got up and dressed, they were offered a breakfast filled with delicacies they had never had before. They were then given a list of chores, which they were more than happy to do.

As Jacob passed the living room, he noticed the same young girl huddled in the corner of the divan. This time, he approached her.

"Hi, my name is Jacob, and I guess I'll be staying here for a while. What is your name?"

She couldn't have been more than a couple of years older than him.

"My name is Greta."

"Do you live here?"

"Yes, my father abandoned me several months ago, and Jordanna found me cold and hungry and took me in. At night, I stay in my room, but during the day, I hardly venture from this spot. Jordanna is very kind and generous. I sometimes help out in the kitchen, but other than that, I don't know what I am going to be doing."

Jacob could not help but feel a certain sadness coming from her. She truly was a lost soul. At least he had Heschel.

It became a morning ritual to stop and see Greta before he went to work. Eventually, Greta would join them and help. Slowly, the sadness began to diminish, and Jacob and Heschel had found a new friend.

The first few weeks at Jordanna's, Jacob became astonished at the change in his life. He had a warm bed to sleep in and more food than he could ever imagine. The opulence he lived in was more than he ever could have envisioned. It was a major comfort to have Heschel to look after. Although he was three years younger than Jacob, Heschel became his comfort.

Both boys would get up in the morning, have a hearty breakfast, and do whatever chores were asked of them. Nothing ever seemed to be too much. Often, Greta would accompany them. They got to know the women. In some respects, it was like having eight or ten mothers. They never actually witnessed what went on behind closed doors, but they understood that it was private and beyond their comprehension.

They worked very hard but had plenty of time for play and relaxation. During the day, some of the women would sit them down and teach them how to read and write. They would tell them stories they had heard about America. The boys became more and more comfortable as time went on and the chicken farm a distant memory.

At one point, Heschel asked Jacob how old they were. This was not such a strange question back then when birthdays were often overlooked by hardworking farmers. The one thing Jacob did understand was that somewhere during the time he had been at Jordanna's, he had turned thirteen. At thirteen, he surely should have been bar mitzvahed. Being thirteen in the Jewish religion was pivotal for a boy; this was his passage into manhood.

Jacob approached Jordanna with this dilemma. Although Jordanna was familiar with this practice, she never really knew what religion she was. Her family never celebrated nor observed any religious holidays. Chaim was definitely a Jew, but he had only daughters, so they never spoke of a bar mitzvah. This was a practice meant only for boys.

When Sarah, the boys' mother, was alive, Sabbath was celebrated every week with the lighting of the Shabbos candles and a hearty dinner. Jacob's heritage was definitely a spark in his being, but since Sarah's death, nothing was ever the same. Religion was never mentioned nor observed. It was almost as if Max was angry at God for taking Sarah.

Jacob now wanted a bar mitzvah. He wasn't quite sure when his birthday was but suggested that since he arrived at Jordanna's on December 10, that would be his birthday. His bar mitzvah was long overdue.

Jordanna understood how important this was to Jacob and brought him to the local rabbi. With all the terror and fear that had become so pervasive in the village, it was a welcome relief to be able to find cause for celebration. Jacob had never been happier. Every afternoon, accompanied by Heschel, Jacob would march to the rabbi's temple, open the Torah, and learn.

Heschel was three years behind but studied along with Jacob so he could help him study when they were at home.

Finally, on a cold February morning, Jacob got up at dawn and with Heschel, Greta, Jordanna, and all the women, as well as some customers, walked themselves to the temple. As they approached the temple, the rabbi could not believe his eyes. Here was a poor farmer's son living in a brothel, yet he commanded so much admiration that everyone wanted to be there to witness this occasion.

The crowd filled the congregation. Mostly all were yawning owing to the very early hour and watched as Jacob covered his shoulders with his talus, wrapped himself with tefillin, and proceeded to open the Torah.

Looking out at the congregation, he became so overwhelmed with pride. "All these people came to see me?"

It was a question he could not fathom. It was at this point that Jacob became so inspired with religion that he made a promise to God and his mother that he would follow the doctrines of the Jewish religion and never go against the rules of the Torah. He pledged himself to God and promised to be a good but humble person. Yes, he truly did become a man on this day.

After a sip of wine, a breaking of the bread, and lots of mazel tov, reality set in. It was a Tuesday morning, and people had to tend to the chores of the day. Jacob would be on cloud nine for the rest of that day and the next and so forth.

Chapter 7

The Incident

Jacob was an observer. As quiet as he was, he was aware of everything around him. He listened, he learned, and he paid attention to all. He got more of an education regarding history, finances, politics, and the climate around him than would have been had if he had been able to attend school.

The men who frequented Jordanna's home liked Jacob. Although he was a poor farmer's son, he had an innate sense of dignity and pride. These men ranged from uneducated poor farmers to men of industry, bankers and officers in the military.

Jacob would often pass women in the street who groveled for a coin or a bit of food. Jacob never put them in the same category as Jordanna's women. He felt very sad for these people but never judged them. He knew Jordanna could not take everyone in. The women in Jordanna's home were respectful and courteous. They may have had a less-than-respectable profession but never acted in a low-class way around the boys. They all helped teach Jacob and Heschel how to read, write, and do whatever math they knew. The men who were regulars at the brothel spoke to Jacob about the ways of the world. He absorbed it all.

By the time the boys had settled into Jordanna's home and felt comfortable enough to consider it their home, a year and half had passed. Jacob was well past his thirteenth birthday and considered himself to be a man, although his life experiences made him more of a man than most much older.

Unrest in the village was growing, and things became even more frightening outside of Jordanna's home. Jacob was not unhappy in this environment. He had his brother, whom he loved dearly, and always felt safe inside these walls.

One year after Jacob arrived, Greta heard from a relative in Sweden who had searched for her. As much as Jacob hated seeing her go, he knew that it would be in her best interest. She had become close with Heschel and him, and when he would pass the empty divan every day, he never felt sad but felt happy for Greta. He would also remind himself that eventually Max would be sending for them.

Then it happened; every feeling of comfort and security would be destroyed by one unsettling, awful event.

One evening, after a very long day, the boys retired to bed early. In the middle of a very deep sleep, Jacob was awakened with the feeling of a hand over his mouth.

Am I dreaming? he thought.

Then the weight of a very large man was on top of his back and pulling at his sleepwear. He was sure he was going to die. He could not breathe, nor could he yell out for help.

Then a pain unlike anything he had ever felt before ripped through him. For the first time, he was hit with a sense of panic that outweighed the pain.

What if I die like this? What will happen to Heschel?

Heschel!

Suddenly, the panic became even more extreme at the thought of what would become of his young brother.

I must be quiet and not wake him.

When the stranger, most likely a Polish soldier, was done with him, he offered up a warning in the most menacing whisper: "If you tell anyone about this, I will come back for your little brother."

The man had the most menacing voice. The only thing that stood out to Jacob was that the man was missing a thumb on his right hand. The man then left, and Jacob never saw his face or recognized his voice as one of Jordanna's regulars.

This one incident was probably the one thing that shaped Jacob's personality from that point on. He became very withdrawn and quiet.

"Oh, Papa!" he would shout at the moon, fists raised. "How could you leave us here in this godforsaken place?"

At night, Jacob slept with a hammer under his pillow. Heschel would become very suspicious about why the door was suddenly barricaded every night. To this, Jacob would explain, "I sleep better knowing that we are alone and together." He said nothing more.

When Jacob would be greeted by the men in Jordanna's home, he listened very carefully as he tried to recognize the voice. He never found out, however, who did this awful, shameful thing to him. He went on about his days but was constantly aware of his surroundings and kept a close eye on Heschel.

Chapter 8

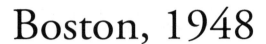

Boston, 1948

"Hello, my landsman. I have heard that you are the best artisan in the city."

That voice. It was a voice he would never forget.

As Jacob stiffened, he slowly turned around to face this new customer. Now he was certain. The one feature Jacob could recognize was the missing thumb. He did all he could do to keep from passing out.

Years had passed since that awful incident, but Jacob never forgot the threatening voice, nor did he ever think he would come face-to-face with that predator. Now it was so many years later, and he was finally able to put a face to the person who had done this shameful thing to him.

Don't be too hasty to react was his first thought.

The hatred welled up in Jacob, but he had to control his emotions. Revenge would be forthcoming, but it had to be methodical. Time would be on his side. After all, Jacob had overcome so much adversity to make a place for himself in America.

By 1948, he was married with three children, had a modest but successful business, and had a great reputation. He was a pillar of his community. At this moment, he felt reduced to rubble but would not let this man get away again. He would have to be cunning and resourceful to get his revenge without jeopardizing his own life.

As Jacob came face-to-face with this monster, he asked "Do I know you?"

The man replied, "No, but you have a great reputation for refurbishing old furniture and making it look new. I have several pieces, and every time I asked for a recommendation, your name came up. I was told you create magic with your skill. Also, it has come to my attention that we come from the same town in Europe. I always like to support my countrymen."

As hard as it was, Jacob smiled and formally introduced himself.

Chapter 9

Jordanna's, 1919

Another year rolled around, and Jacob was a changed man. By now, he was turning fifteen, and Max finally sent for his boys. He had made a good life for himself in America. He had met and married a woman named Esther, and together, they owned a home on a chicken farm. The eggs made a good profit, and they used some of that money to put a small general store on the property. It was now time for the boys to come home to America.

Jacob envisioned a wonderful life in a new land with a new mother whom he hoped had tamed his father. He dreamed of going to school and learning English. There was no end to how far he could go in America. He could finally put all the evil behind him and start a new life. Little did he know how wrong he was.

Through the excitement of going to America, there was trepidation. Jacob had become accustomed to living in Jordanna's home with Heschel. For a boy the age of fifteen, he had grown up quickly, although not by choice. The women had been very kind and taught the boys how to read, write, and learn the ways of the world. Much of what the boys were exposed to had nothing to do with a proper education.

Jacob was a pragmatic person who saw much but said little. He took everything in and learned well. Although the world around them was crumbling with terror and rumors of pogroms, the boys were comfortable with the knowledge that they knew what they had but were fearful of the mystery abroad. Max had never been a caring father and never showed compassion or empathy. The thought of seeing him again after all these years did nothing to soothe the boys' fear of the unknown.

Why did Mama have to die so young? thought Jacob.

She would have given the boys a home, with love and care. Now at twelve and fifteen, they were facing a long trip abroad to America on a ship filled with strangers. Jacob was still just a boy but had been forced to become a man at a very young age.

There was much talk among the men who visited Jordanna's home on a regular basis of a war breaking out in America. One such man, Zev, had become close to Jacob—well, as close as Jacob was to anyone.

Zev was astonished to hear that Jacob and Heschel were to sail to America.

"Change your passage immediately," he told the boys. "There is a great war about to break out all over America, and you must change your passage to Cuba instead."

The boys were still very young and had no idea about the ways of the world. Jacob was frightened by Zev's outcry. With their last bit of money, Jacob did what was suggested.

Jordanna, upon finding out what Jacob had done, was furious. She had, after all, promised Max that she would keep the boys safe until he sent for them. Going to Cuba was not part of the plan. Besides, if America was to go to war, it would not be on American soil.

By now, the boys had changed their plans and had no more money to change the tickets again. The ship to America was leaving in three days. Being a person with many contacts, some not so honest, Jordanna managed to get the boys' visas stamped so that they were back on the ship to America. Jacob had never felt so displaced, but he trusted Jordanna more than anyone else.

The day finally arrived when Jacob and Heschel would be leaving Jordanna. She had become a surrogate mother to these boys (now young men), and it was a difficult parting for all. Jacob pleaded with Jordanna to come with them, but her home and her roots were here. In spite of impending war and terrible crimes being committed to so many around her, she still felt safe in her environment. She had developed lasting friendships with the people who frequented her home and could not fathom leaving that.

With a very heavy heart, she packed up food and drink and brought the boys to the train station. For Jacob, it was another major loss in his life. The excitement of his journey ahead was buried beneath the anguish he felt.

Chapter 10

The Voyage

The train ride from Koretz to Gdansk was bumpy and noisy. Jacob felt a great deal of responsibility for his younger brother. Other than that awful and fateful night at Jordanna's, the past three years were filled with a life that he would never have known. The house was large and comfortable, the people friendly, and food plentiful. He learned much from the patrons and developed a kind and gentle spirit from the women.

Jacob and Heschel were now embarking on an unknown journey. The excitement, however, was clouded with the knowledge that they would most likely never see Jordanna again.

Max was a mean and tyrannical man when they saw him last. Perhaps his new wife in a new country had softened him. This hope was foremost in Jacob's mind.

The train was crowded with wall-to-wall people: babies crying and people shoving and pushing. When the train finally stopped at the port in Gdansk, the boys could not get off fast enough. Fortunately, Jordanna had provided a sufficient amount of food for their journey so their stomachs were full.

The authorities from America and the steamship line quickly gave Jacob and Heschel numbers and directed them to a long line. The ship was not to leave port until the following day, but before they could board, they had to be examined for any disease or infection. Even a slight cough could ruin their chances of getting on the ship.

There was a sea of people waiting in long lines, and some would not get through. Hours and hours had passed before Jacob and Heschel finally finished all inspections and delousing. Jacob thought often about his illegal papers that ended up being forged. He feared that someone would notice each time he had to present them.

Finally finished with all questions and exams, the boys were put in a holding room to wait all night for boarding in the morning.

At dawn, they were escorted—mostly pushed—through a large door onto a dock. It was *the* boat. A ship larger than life. Jacob had never seen anything like it before. It was a city on water. People were struggling, anxious to get on board, but there were restrictions. Another meeting with medical staff came first, then questions about who would be receiving them in America. Although the boys had their father, they were still very ignorant of the ways of the world. All they knew was that Max was in Boston, Massachusetts, USA. Beyond that, they knew nothing.

Oy ve, Jacob thought. *Bring me back to Jordanna's. What are we doing?*

Finally, the boys boarded the ship and were escorted to steerage. This was composed of many cots lined up, some hovering over each other. The human stench was already stifling, and they hadn't even left port yet.

The realization that they would be here for three-plus weeks terrified Jacob. After all, they were used to the finery of Jordanna's home. Here they were, surrounded by hundreds of strangers and crying children. What could be worse? Thankfully, the exhaustion of the past two weeks crept up, and after finding their assigned spaces, they both fell into a sound sleep.

It couldn't have been long before a long, loud siren blasted. This was the captain's way of getting everyone's attention. His instructions were very clear.

The ship consisted of three distinct classes. The highest levels were for first class, the center levels were for second class, and the lowest level was for third class, or better known as steerage. The captain was very clear that each passenger was to stay on the decks they were assigned to. They could venture out onto the deck that was considered part of third class but were not to go any higher. They would be served food and drink, and responsibility for keeping their quarters clean was solely on them. Any suspicion of sickness had to be reported.

Jacob could not help but remember that he was, after all, a poor chicken farmer's son. The past three years were spent in the lap of luxury, but the reality was, he was still Max's son.

Fortunately, although Jacob and Heschel were in steerage, there were only 90 passengers on their level. There were 576 passengers on the ship in total, most of them being in first class. Jacob and Heschel were able to carve out a niche for themselves with the hope that the time would pass quickly and the seas would be calm. It was, after all, a new adventure.

Finally, the horn from the ship blasted long and loud. They were leaving the homeland they knew and were embarking on an unknown journey. They quickly raced to the outside deck and stayed and watched until the shoreline became a tiny thread in the horizon.

So many emotions overcame Jacob. He was, after all, only fifteen years old but had lived a lifetime. He had no idea of what would await him. What was America like? Would it be welcoming? Would his *father* be welcoming? After all, he had not seen him in three years, and the only emotion he knew was fear of him. He could not honestly say that he loved his father or even knew him. Jacob hoped beyond hope that his father was now a changed man and would open a warm, inviting heart to his sons.

Day 1

The boys were so exhausted from the long journey to get to the ship that sleep came easy the night before. During the day, they busied themselves with lessons that Jordanna had provided them with and walks around the designated areas. The sea was calm, and the promise of an easy journey seemed to be possible. Trust did not come easy to Jacob, making forming friendly relationships with other passengers unlikely.

Day 2

The seas were beginning to get a little rough, and the stench from other passengers retching was overwhelming. Most had never travelled on water before, and seasickness was rampant.

The second night was a little more difficult to handle. Crying babies and coughing men and women made the noise level intolerable. Jacob and Heschel spent most of the day outside and busied themselves with looking out for whales or dolphins.

Days 3–7

The next several days went without incident, and the boys seemed to fall into a routine: get up, eat breakfast, roam the deck, work on lessons, and look for whales. The time seemed to pass easily, but still, they kept to themselves and spoke to no one.

By the second week, other passengers were beginning to get short-tempered. Accusations were flying, although none directed at Jacob or Heschel.

It was toward the end of the second week that screams were heard late at night. An officer from the shipping line came running in and pulled a grubby old man off a young teenage girl. Memories came flooding back to Jacob, and fear and depression set in. Heschel never knew what had happened to him at Jordanna's home, and Jacob could not explain it to him now.

The next few days seemed to drag on endlessly. Jacob and Heschel found that staying out on deck was much better than staying in their quarters. The seas were bumpy, and people were retching overboard one after the other. Making friends on this cruise was not an option. Everyone was suspicious of everyone else. Any belongings had to be watched over constantly. No one could be trusted. Everyone on this ship was looking for a better life in America. If this was any indication of what was to come, then America was no better than what they were leaving.

The last few days were agonizing. Rumors of other passengers passing away on board abounded. Several passengers were separated from their families and put into quarantine. The knowledge that they may have to be sent back on the next ship was terrifying. What of the rest of their families? The quarters were either too cold or too hot. Everyone was claustrophobic. It was clear that some were sick and afraid to admit it. And then...

A sight so beautiful, so astounding appeared. The ship was approaching New York, and the Statue of Liberty seemed to appear out of nowhere. It seemed to be welcoming everyone on board to their new lives in America.

Seeing this vision, a calmness came over Jacob, and the knowledge that he would be home with his new family, albeit including his father, made the journey worth it. Little did he know what would be facing him.

Heschel grabbed on to Jacob and held on for dear life. They had made it! They would be getting off this vessel and would be able to breathe in clean American air. The emotions were flying high. Over and over again, Heschel would exclaim, "We made it!"

Of course, arriving at Ellis Island did not necessarily mean America was welcoming them with open arms.

Chapter 11

Welcome to America

Once again, the lines were forming, the documents being stamped, and the doctors examining. It was then that Jacob's breathing did not pass the test. With the doctors fearful of tuberculosis, Jacob was placed in quarantine. Heschel was separated and placed in a detention center until it could be determined whether or not to send Jacob back.

All their hopes and dreams were quashed. Heschel had never been without Jacob before. Jacob had never been unable to care for Heschel. The fear of the unknown came back to haunt both of them. Jacob was very aware that he was holding down a cough on most of the trip. He also knew that if he let it be known that he was not well, he most definitely would risk never getting off the ship. He would wait until Heschel fell asleep most nights and go out on deck. The moist air from the sea was soothing, and the sounds of the engines and the waves muffled any coughing he let out. Now he had finally made it to America, and the thought that all this may have been for nothing was frightening.

The nurses and caretakers in quarantine were short-tempered and nasty. They viewed all these people as dirty immigrants bringing disease into their country. Jacob was petrified. Where was Heschel? He could barely contain his emotions until one day, when a kind, friendly smile appeared.

Am I dreaming? he thought.

"Hello, Jacob."

It was a new volunteer whom he had never seen before. A human with a heart.

She took Jacob's hand and felt his pulse. After checking his fever, she patted his arm and told him that whatever had ailed him to bring him to this point seemed to be over. He had no fever, his pulse had slowed, and his breathing was no longer shallow. His time in quarantine would soon be over.

She spent some time with Jacob and let him know that her family had arrived recently so she understood what Jacob had been going through. She volunteered her time at this clinic to soothe the fear that these people had of being sent back. She spoke Yiddish, which was the language Jacob knew best.

She introduced herself as Elizabeth. Although she had been born in this country, she was first generation, and most of her aunts and uncles were still in Eastern Europe. Her grandparents had come over recently, and they were hoping to get the rest of the family over shortly.

This angel created a calmness in Jacob that he had never before experienced. For the first time in his life, small bursts of joy entered his soul. He was well versed in female-male relationships but had still not experienced the kind of emotion that he was experiencing now when Elizabeth was there.

It was the first time since arriving that Jacob had a moment of peace and slept well. Thoughts of Elizabeth raced through his mind. She was the one thing that made his time in quarantine bearable. He went to sleep every night looking forward to Elizabeth's visits the following day. For the first time, he was not in a rush to leave quarantine.

Elizabeth spent many hours with Jacob learning of his background. He had never before opened up so much of his life to anyone—all but that most shameful time at Jordanna's. Jacob could not believe it himself. She was so easy to talk to. He was just shy of sixteen but appeared so much older. Elizabeth was seventeen and still studying for her nursing degree but put everything on hold to volunteer at Ellis Island as long as these ships loaded with immigrants were still coming.

Jacob explained to her that his brother was placed in another area of the island, and she offered to find him and let him know how Jacob was doing. She would return with news of Heschel. Knowing that Heschel was okay and being cared for soothed Jacob's heart, and he finally relaxed.

Jacob spent thirty days in quarantine. Except for the first week, most of his time there was spent getting to know Elizabeth. They were never out of things to talk about. During that time, Max's distant cousin in New York City would check in on Heschel. Until it was determined that Jacob did not have a communicable disease, Heschel was in a holding pattern and could not leave the island. If truth be known, he didn't want to leave without Jacob anyhow.

Had it not been for Heschel, Jacob would have found a way to stay on Ellis Island. He was so smitten with Elizabeth and found it so hard to leave her. He was inclined to believe that his feelings were returned. Time flowed easily whenever Elizabeth was around. She never seemed to be in a rush to leave Jacob's side any more than Jacob wanted her to. They quickly formed a bond that made the thought of leaving her unbearable for Jacob.

Before he left, Jacob got the name and contact information of the wonderful angel who had cared for him. Somehow, somewhere, he knew he would have to see her again. Maybe there would be hope in America, after all.

A spark had been ignited in Jacob, one that he could not put out.

Chapter 12

❦

A New Country

When it was finally determined that Jacob did not have tuberculosis and could enter the country, all documents were stamped, and Jacob and Heschel began their journey to Boston, Massachusetts.

First, they had to take the ferry into the city, and their jaws dropped at the sight of the huge buildings. Their imagination could not have conjured up such a sight. So many people, so many big buildings. Automobiles honking their horns. The noise was deafening but somehow soothing. Life was being lived all around them.

Jacob and Heschel wished they could have stayed and just observe, but they had a train to catch. There was no joy at the thought of seeing their father after all this time. Their only hope was that his new wife had somehow tamed him.

They discussed several scenarios on the trip to Boston. Most of them were speckled with hope of a happy homelife. They envisioned being greeted by a warm and comforting woman who would now be their mother. Max would be a changed man and would be welcoming his boys with open arms. How he had missed them. They would all move into the house on the farm and work the small store Max had opened. Jacob and Heschel would go to school and learn English.

Jacob's hope of eventually going to college was clear in his mind. He had a thirst for knowledge, and America would offer all these opportunities to him. Yes, their hopes and dreams were laid out on the train to Boston. Nothing could stop them. Added to this was

Jacob's thoughts of Elizabeth. He was too inexperienced to notice the signs that Elizabeth was sad to see him go. He just knew that a spark had begun, and he wanted the opportunity to see her again.

There was no clear route from New York to Boston at this time, so it was necessary to change trains often. The various train stations intrigued the boys. Some seemed to be in remote places with farms around and many horses and carriages. People were dressed mostly in overalls and boots and seemed to keep their heads down and focus on what the moment was bringing.

The environment reminded Jacob more of the essence of home. At some point, the population would be heavy, women in long dresses, men in jackets and cravats. The looks on their faces were more jovial and seemed to represent a more relaxed presence. Both the women's hairdos and clothing were not like anything Jacob had seen before. It was a new era, a new country, and, most of all, a new way of life.

Jacob liked these stops. It gave him an opportunity to stretch his legs and observe. This trip was a lot more interesting than that horrible boat ride overseas. Jacob realized early on that the click-clack of the trains on the rails had different sounds on every train. In his mind, he composed a symphony: "First I will learn English, then the violin."

He sang this over and over in his mind. One of Jordanna's patrons had become very fond of Jacob and had given him a small violin as a going-away gift. Also, he was instructed to play for the chickens. The patron believed that the music would soothe the chickens and their eggs would be much sweeter.

Finally, the conductor yelled out, "Next stop, Boston! Everyone get ready to disembark."

At this, Jacob's heart beat so loud and so hard that he thought it was going to jump out of his body. For Heschel's sake, however, he had to put up a good front and make this a new adventure—a *good* adventure.

As they gathered their scant belongings and left the train, Heschel and Jacob approached the platform. They looked all around and saw nothing nor anyone familiar.

So many people. So much noise. Had Papa forgotten us? Jacob's heart dropped.

The conductor told them that they must walk to the end of the platform, and sure enough, there, at the end of the platform, was Max, their father.

The years had apparently not softened him. There were no out-stretched arms, no smile on his face, no apparent mellowing in his heart.

Standing next to him was an equally stern-looking woman. Clearly, she was bursting with child.

Upon seeing the boys, Max yelled out, "Hurry, hurry, we must get going! This is my wife, Esther. She is your new mother, and you will mind what she says. Come, let's get you home, and we'll all get something to eat."

Oy Gevalt, Jacob thought. *More than three years had gone by without him seeing his children, and this is the greeting we get?*

Heschel could not take his eyes off his brother's face, looking for some sign of encouragement. What he saw was disappointment and confusion. How does a father who has not seen his children in such a long time not show some sort of emotion upon laying his eyes on them?

"I see Jordanna took good care of you. Is she well? Did you behave in her care?" Obviously, she was Max's main concern.

Esther pushed them along.

"We must get home and get settled."

Max had his old, rickety pickup truck parked outside.

Jacob was very excited to see the farm with the store on the property and asked Max how long the ride would be. With that, Max actually let out a laugh and let Jacob know that there was no farm, no store, no chickens. Yes, it was in his plans for the future, someday, but for now, there was only a small apartment in the West End of Boston. Heschel was young enough to go to school, but Jacob would have to find a job and move out. He was expected to be on his own. If he wanted to go to school to learn English, it would have to be at night and on his own time.

By the time they got into Max's beat-up pickup truck, all of Jacob's dreams of a better life were quashed. It took years and miles and tons of travels to plan his dreams and desires but only minutes to beat it down. Hadn't he suffered enough? At sixteen years old, he had grown in so many ways. He would never get to be a child or get to be treated like one. Max was a very hateful, nasty man.

For now though, Jacob realized that he was a stranger in a strange land and would have to rely on Max to get him through his days. He resented this as much as he resented this horrible person being his father. The realization set in that Jacob would have to be responsible for navigating his own life here on in. Heschel would have to learn to deal with Max and Esther as best he could. Life as they all knew it was completely over.

Jacob was always the observer, and now he needed to observe more than ever. The customs were different, the language was different, the currency was totally foreign to him. Yes, he had lots to absorb.

Chapter 13

Strange Boy in a Strange Town

For the first two weeks in Boston, Jacob stayed with Max and Esther. The apartment was crowded; however, Jacob and Heschel found some comfort in being together no matter how uncomfortable the living conditions were. During the day, Max would leave for work and take Jacob with him. He worked in a local factory loading and unloading cartons onto a truck. Jacob would work alongside him, and for this, he would get paid a small stipend.

The men in the factory liked Jacob and helped him as much as they could. They taught him some English and helped him figure out where he could find a low-rent rooming house with decent living conditions. Clearly, Max was of little help. His main concern was to get Jacob out on his own so that he and Esther could have back whatever little space they already had. Of course, Heschel was still there, but they rationalized that he could be a big help around the house and could run errands for Esther. After all, she was getting larger by the day with child, and moving around was not easy for an already-buxom woman.

By the third week, Jacob had figured out the lay of the land and discovered that a room had opened up in a boardinghouse that one of the factory men was living in. His salary from the factory just about covered his rent and food expense. At night, he attended classes to help his English.

Fortunately, Jacob was very smart and caught on quickly. His passion for learning was great, but the tragedy of it was the fact that he could not attend classes to further his education and work at the same time. At times, it felt as though Max had taken him from the smoke and placed him into the fire. Everyone kept saying that America was the land of opportunity, and with that thought in mind, Jacob would prevail and be patient until his time would come.

Jacob had been in America for a little over a month and was starting to get familiar with his surroundings. He would venture from work to class to home. At times, he would be invited to Max's for a meal and to visit with Heschel, but basically, he was on his own. Mainly, he would see Heschel on weekends and show him around the areas of Boston he had become familiar with. He cherished these times.

Heschel was enrolled in school and found that there were many boys like him who had emigrated to America and, like him, did not speak the language or know the customs. The instructors worked with these immigrants to speed along their learning process, and he learned rapidly. When Heschel was with his brother, they would share what they were learning and would make a game of it. Boston was a long way from Koretz in every way.

When it was time to separate, the boys were miserable. They had been through so much together but were now having to experience such an important part of their lives individually with no support.

Heschel spoke unkindly of Esther. She seemed to be a female extension of Max. Apparently, he had met his match. She never let an opportunity pass to berate Heschel and let him know that as soon as he was of age, he would also follow in his brother's footsteps. He always felt that he was an unwelcome burden to his own father. In many ways, Jacob was better off being on his own. He would see his father at work, but even there, Max showed him no more attention, nor did he give him any more thought as he would to any other worker.

Chapter 14

❦

Molasses, Molasses Everywhere

By January, Jacob had been in the country for several months. On this particular day, the temperature outside was unseasonably comfortable, and Jacob took this opportunity to take a stroll during one of his breaks from work. The previous week had been very cold, and venturing outdoors was not a good option.

As he was approaching Commercial Street, loud sirens were blaring and people were running everywhere.

What could have happened? he asked himself.

The air was noxious, thick with a pungent odor. People were screaming, and all he could think of was that they were being attacked. After all, hadn't Jordanna's friend warned him of an imminent war in America?

Jacob quickly ran back to work to find out that a molasses tank fifty feet tall containing almost 2.5 million gallons of molasses had ruptured and molasses was running through the streets of the North End. A twenty-five-foot-high wave of molasses moving at 35 mph was ripping buildings off their foundations and damaging the girders from the elevated train system.

The Boston Post reported later that day that several blocks were flooded to a depth of two to three feet of molasses. The body count had not yet been determined, and the number of people injured was vast. All Jacob could think of was how fortunate he was to not have been fifteen minutes earlier, or he would have been in the center of this catastrophic event.

In the end, there were 21 people dead, and another 150 were injured. Fortunately, a training ship from the Massachusetts Nautical School was nearby. One hundred sixteen cadets raced to the scene along with the Boston police, nurses, Red Cross, Army, and other personnel. They worked through the night, sometimes diving into the molasses to rescue people. The molasses was waist deep, which made the rescue a nearly impossible struggle.

No one could ever have imagined such a tragedy. The rupture of the tank was blamed on the sudden rise of external temperature. Although the unseasonably warmer day was delightful to many people, the sudden rise in temperature caused the tank to expand and weaken.

Thus prompted Jacob's curiosity about how environment's control has a responsibility to everything in life aside from the weather. It can interact with metal in one instance, wood in another. It seemed that the world was affected by environmental changes. He vowed that he would learn everything he could about this and apply it to his craft.

Jacob had been through so much in his life. He looked at his survival through this awful event as an opportunity. He had managed to be so close to such an awful situation, but at the same time, he avoided being caught up in it.

His cup was suddenly half-full. He could have looked at this as another negative force in his life, but he had survived.

Chapter 15

A Well-Learned Young Man

Jacob was attending classes in English at the local community center. With his newfound interest in change and effect due to the environment, he would stay late and read as much as he could absorb about climate and its effects.

It was also where he met and befriended Saul. Saul was an upholsterer and master craftsman with wood in the Old Country and was trying to make a go of it in America. He had taken a liking to Jacob and offered to teach him the trade. The pay would be low, but it was still comparable to what he was making now, and he would learn a trade. Lifting and lowering heavy cartons was certainly not going to get him anything but a bad back. He would also not have to come face-to-face with Max on a daily basis as a reminder of what a nasty individual his father was. Yes, he had survived in order to live and learn in America.

By spring, Jacob's English was coming along well. He was able to keep a conversation going, and since he was such a fast learner, he was able to learn his new trade. He and Saul became fast friends, and they enjoyed working together. When possible, he would visit Heschel on weekends and take him on field trips. Eventually, the field trips would end up back in Saul's shop, and Saul would find himself with two students. He couldn't afford to pay both of them but would hand Heschel a few coins every now and then, making Heschel enjoy the time together even more.

During the week, Jacob began attending classes to become an American citizen. Yes, life in America was looking up. Keeping his distance from Max and Esther was also a plus.

By now, Esther had delivered her baby, and this consumed her entire life. Instead of treating the boys as her new baby's brothers, she pretty much excluded them from the baby's life. She had one child, a little boy whom she named David, and smothered him with all the nurturing she was capable of. Certainly, there was nothing left for Heschel or Jacob. Max was busy working to support his wife and new baby and had little time left for Heschel when he came home, anyway.

Heschel looked forward to the day that he would be able to leave and live with Jacob. Heschel never forgot the vision of his mother being placed in the ground and often wondered how she could have lived with such a mean man. His and Jacob's lives would have been so different had Sarah lived. She would have protected and loved her sons and kept them from Max's fury. At least Heschel could find solace in knowing that his brother, whom he had shared so much with, was nearby and would someday be able to spend his days with him once again.

In the meantime, Jacob was continuing to bring Heschel to Saul's workroom on weekends. Jacob was becoming a talented upholsterer under Saul's tutelage and found he was developing a following. He loved his work so much that he always worked with a smile and a handshake. Saul's shop was getting busier and busier, and ultimately, Saul found that he needed to move to a larger space. He found a new, larger shop with two apartments over it. He quickly took it and moved himself, along with his new bride, and Jacob into both places. Jacob was moving up in this world and was taking Heschel along with him.

The one dark spot in Jacob's life was still his father. He had not changed at all. He was still grumpy, curt and offered the boys no assistance. Heschel was finding it intolerable to live with him and Esther. She was equally as mean as her husband. Since she had delivered her baby, it was all she cared about. She smothered him with any love and attention she had. She made the boys very much aware that the bloodline stopped there. The infant was her flesh and blood, and even though the three boys shared the same father, nothing was as strong as the bond between mother and child. Esther did not even try to connect with the boys in a meaningful way.

Thus began the strained relationship Heschel and Jacob would always have with their half-brother, David. Through the years, nothing ever changed. There was to always be a sense of superiority with David, but if truth be told, Heschel and Jacob were much better off being on their own. Their lives would be much happier without the shadow of Esther constantly over them.

Chapter 16

Settling In

The first two years Jacob spent in America seemed to be a peaceful time. He loved working with Saul and loved working in the furniture business. His mind was like a sponge and absorbed information and facts on almost all topics. This also assisted him in making the right decisions for his clients regarding the way various fabrics would respond to different climates. He would sound so knowledgeable that even Saul would come to him for advice.

Several boys he had known in the "old country" came over on the ship with him and had landed in the same area Jacob was in. They also ended up in the textile industry and remained very close with Jacob. This was not so much a coincidence as one would think.

Little by little, new relationships formed, and everyone who came in contact with Jacob admired his honesty and integrity. He was a friend to all. At night, he, along with his brother, would attend classes to improve their English. He would never lose his accent, but somehow, this was what endeared him to many people to begin with. He may have been small in stature—he was actually not more than five feet four—but he was a giant when it came to respect. He gave it to all who was deserving and in return got it back many times over. He was a quiet, shy, small man who did not make any waves and, therefore, stayed out of everyone's business.

The one thing he treasured most of all was his violin that he had brought over from Poland. It reminded him of Jordanna, and he often wondered where she was and how she would be doing. He wasn't able to accomplish much with his musical instrument, but he valued it more than any other possession he had. He did not realize it at the time, but Max abandoning his boys was probably the best thing that could have happened to them. They were schooled in a way that was superior to any classroom they could have attended.

As soon as Heschel was able to, he moved in with Jacob, and they relished their small apartment over the furniture repair shop. At this time, there were so many people immigrating to America that Boston was becoming a melting pot of languages and customs. Eventually, it seemed that all Jews landed in one district, the Italians in another, and still the Irish and Asians landed in their own niche. This developed the various sections that were coarsely mapped out over the city. Small shuls rose up in the West End of Boston, allowing people to get together and reminisce about their days in East Europe. Typically, people stayed in their designated areas, and strong bonds were formed.

Eventually, Max actually did purchase the chicken farm in the country. He was able to get five acres of land in Millis, Massachusetts, and not only put in his chicken coops but also build a small grocery store in front of the farm. The property came with a small house on two levels, and David had the luxury of running around the property playing with the chickens and fetching eggs. Not much, if any, of this time had anything to do with Jacob or Heschel.

Several years passed without much hardship. Jacob and Heschel became proficient in English, and much of their shyness melted away. Elizabeth, however, was never far from Jacob's mind. He longed for the day that he would have enough courage to try to reach out to her.

The boys would always be on the quiet side, always remaining the observant. Jacob wasn't making a lot of money as an upholsterer, but his reputation for doing excellent work spread. He made a living and bought himself his first car. The only downside to this was that he was expected to make a weekly trek every Sunday to Millis. This had more to do with helping Max out than sharing paternal affection. Jacob and Heschel may have been offered a cup of tea with a slice of bread, but never more than that. Neither lunch nor dinner was ever offered.

As time passed, Saul, who was much older than the boys, decided to move on. The cold winters were bothering his bones, and he and his wife decided to sell the building and move to a warmer climate. The West End was booming, and property values were rising. Jacob could not afford to buy the building from Saul, but he needed a shop to work out of. This prompted Jacob and Heschel to open a small store front in another part of Boston that was more affordable and continue the craft that they learned so well.

Chapter 17

A Bold Move

Jacob was a fast learner, and English became his primary language. When alone with his brother, he would often revert to Yiddish but would catch himself and make Heschel speak English as well.

As well as things were going, there was always a void in Jacob's life. He thought often of Elizabeth and convinced himself that there could be no one but her in his life. With this thought in mind, he set out to find her. He was now a shop owner with a car and a steady but modest income. It was time.

Jacob kept Elizabeth's information stored in a special spot and would look at it often. This time, he picked up the phone and began to call. Just as suddenly, he put the phone down and thought again, *What if she doesn't remember me? What if she's married? What if…* Anything.

As he looked at her address, it occurred to him that a letter would be the best way to contact her. Even if she no longer lived at the same address, perhaps the postal service could forward it. Also, it would be less of a shock and would give her time to ponder and perhaps remember him.

With that thought in mind, Jacob sat down and wrote the following:

Dear Elizabeth,

It has been several years since I left Ellis Island, but I will never forget your kindness. It was your smile and compassion that got me through that awful time in my life.

I have settled in Boston and have my own business now. Things have definitely turned out fine. I was wondering if there could be a possibility of seeing you again. I will understand if you do not remember me. It has been a while, and I'm sure thousands of men like me have gone through your ward.

I have my own automobile and would love to drive into New York to see you again. Please let me know if this is a possibility.

I look forward to your reply,
Jacob Kalinsky

It had not even occurred to Jacob that Elizabeth could be married by now, have a family, or not even live in New York anymore. Jacob was so smitten with her that he never even thought to look at other women. Dating was actually something foreign to him. It's odd that with his background he was so inept at knowing anything about the opposite sex. The only thing he knew was that he had met a woman who brought to the surface certain feelings for him that he never knew existed. He had to at least try to find out what that was all about. With that in mind, Jacob ran to the post office and mailed off the letter, making certain that his return address was on the envelope. Now he had to wait.

Jacob would run to his mailbox every day, to no avail. Finally, three weeks went by, and the return address on the envelope in his mailbox was unmistakable. No one, not even Heschel, had any idea what Jacob was up to. He had never discussed his feelings with anyone.

Now he had this envelope in his hand and had to contain his excitement. Ridden with fear and excitement at the same time, Jacob put the unopened envelope in his pocket. He wanted to wait until he got home, pour a whiskey, and gingerly open the letter from Elizabeth.

Chapter 18

The Letter

The day seemed to drag by. All Jacob could concentrate on was the letter. As long as he did not open it, he could fantasize what the contents said. His hope was that Elizabeth was alive and well and thought of him from time to time as well. Of course, his dream could be totally shattered at the thought of total rejection, or worse. She could be married or could have contracted a fatal illness while at Ellis Island. None of these scenarios were out of the question.

Jacob came so close to opening the letter while still at work, but his discipline forbade it. He would count the hours, proceed home, and follow through with his plan to relax with a schnapps in his hand and clear his mind.

At last, Jacob was home, alone, and could breathe. He gingerly opened the letter and braced himself for the first sentence:

Dear Jacob,

I cannot begin to tell you how shocked, amazed, and thrilled I was to hear from you. Yes, it's been several years, but I felt so close to you during our short time together at Ellis Island and never seemed inclined to make that connection again.

Shortly after you left, I developed tuberculosis and spent much of the following year in quarantine and sometimes near death. Believe it or not, I spent many hours recapping the conversations we had and hoped that when, or if, I got better, I would somehow find you.

So many thousands of people from Eastern Europe came through Ellis that year and the next. I did recover but found the possibility of finding you daunting. So many names were changed going through immigration.

I returned to nursing school and lost myself in my studies. I have devoted the past few years taking care of the many people who have come from abroad and dedicated my life to my profession. Never have I met anyone else nor have I been interested in developing a romantic relationship with anyone. Then your letter arrived, and my heart burst with hope and happiness.

I suppose in a normal situation, people take more time to get to know each other, but in the short time we had, I felt that we developed a strong bond. Of course, this could have been in my mind only, and you might not have given me another thought. So much time has gone by, and the hope of ever seeing you again had diminished.

I am so happy and proud of all you have accomplished in your time in this country. It can be a warm, welcoming place, but it can also become cold and lonely. I am thrilled that it is the former.

I am posting my current address and phone number. I am still in New York but will anxiously await to hear from you and look forward to seeing you very soon.

My fondest regards,
Elizabeth

Jacob could hardly contain his happiness. Never in his wildest dreams did he really think he would once again see Elizabeth. He wanted it desperately but was afraid to hope. Now he had a way to see her again. His heart soared, but his body shook with trepidation. What if he was not what she remembered? What if her disappointment was so apparent that he would shy away in shame? To imagine a great reunion was more than he could hope for.

Heschel? Jacob had never mentioned Elizabeth to him, and suddenly, he would be running to New York City to see her? How could he make Heschel understand that up until now Elizabeth was more a figment of his imagination than real? This conversation could not be put off.

That evening, Jacob sat Heschel down and told him everything that had gone on while he was on Ellis Island. He explained that an angel sent by God had rescued him from despair and he was now going to make it his plan to see her again. She had never been out of his thoughts.

Heschel was surprised but very excited and happy for Jacob. He encouraged him to do whatever was necessary to be with this woman again.

Jacob was elated. One more hurdle was jumped. It was all happening so fast, albeit several years had passed.

Chapter 19

Unchartered Waters

Jacob had never had a romantic relationship with a woman. He barely knew how to speak to the opposite sex without his nerves getting the best of him; this is why his ability to open up to Elizabeth so easily both surprised and gladdened him. Now he was faced with the dilemma of what would be the best way to contact her. A letter would take too long, but a telegraph would be quick and alleviate the nervousness a phone conversation would present.

As soon as he could, he ran down to the telegraph office and replied to Elizabeth's letter.

> Dear Elizabeth,
>
> I was so happy to hear from you. In response, I would like to meet you in New York City. Please let me know when and where. I so look forward to seeing you again.
>
> Jacob Kalinsky

Before he could think twice, Jacob quickly sent the telegram. His heart was beating out of his chest. Once more, he found himself on the waiting side. Elizabeth's response could not come fast enough.

Jacob spent the next few days immersed in work. He had become known for his knowledge regarding cause and effect with materials and metals. This was fortuitous because had Jacob been able to attend college, his interests would have been geared for chemistry. The molasses explosion ignited an innate curiosity into the whys and hows of everything man-made. Here was a poor chicken farmer's son who was destined for nothing great, who was now respected—no, revered—for his passion for learning.

Yes, America was a wonderful country where if you worked hard you could make it. Of course, being the kindhearted and generous soul that Jacob was, he would sooner give it away rather than use his knowledge for material gain. No, he would never be cash rich, but in his world, he was rich in the things that mattered. He was still young enough to continue his craft and study on the side as well. Word was getting around that this talented artisan was as knowledgeable as well as talented with his hands.

By the fifth day after sending the telegraph, Jacob was becoming concerned.

What if I was too eager? he would ask himself. *Maybe Elizabeth was frightened by my forwardness.*

At any rate, the time seemed to drag on.

By day 7, the letter arrived:

Dear Jacob,

I was once again happy to receive your telegraph. I would like to see you again and can arrange a meeting for next Sunday. I would love to show you the city.

Please let me know if you are driving or taking the train here. We can meet on the Lower East Side, which is where I now live. My address, as you know, is 76 Eldridge Street.

If you arrive Saturday night after Sabbath, you can stay in a small rooming house down the street. That way, we will have all day Sunday to spend together. I imagine we have a lot to catch up on.

Please let me know if you want me to make these arrangements for you.

I so look forward to seeing you again.

Elizabeth

Jacob's heart was doing triple time. "She wants to see me." He let out a very long sigh. It was as though he had been holding his breath ever since sending the telegraph.

Jacob immediately responded with a resounding yes, although not wanting to seem too eager, the resounding sound was held back. He planned to drive to New York on Saturday night, stay over at the rooming house, and take Elizabeth for a fine breakfast Sunday morning. Heschel would be left with the responsibility of explaining to Max why he could not be there on Sunday. Jacob respected Max because he was his father, but for no other reason. He had never done anything to earn his son's respect or love, and Jacob was not going to spend another minute doing his bidding.

Jacob had never before felt such joy. It was only Tuesday. How would he get through the following four days?

On Wednesday morning, Jacob awoke with a beaming smile on his face. Most people were not accustomed to seeing him like this. He was not a sullen person but a serious man who was not prone to laughter. Nothing could shake his spirit now. He was a new person with a goal, and nothing or no one was going to ruin this feeling. Sunday could not come fast enough.

Fortunately, work was keeping his mind occupied. He had a steady flow of customers coming and going into his shop. Everyone noticed a drastic change in Jacob, and most did comment on it. He was actually jovial. Even Heschel got caught up in Jacob's happiness. He was so happy for his brother. Maybe America would be the best thing that happened to both of them. He could not wait for this weekend to be over to hear the stories that Jacob would come home with. Mostly, he was excited for this new chapter in his brother's life.

The only question that remained was how Max would react to the news that Jacob would not be there on Sunday. This would be a job that Heschel would have to ruminate over long and hard before he got to Max and Esther's on Sunday.

Chapter 20

The Trip

Saturday finally came. Although Jacob was a religious man, he could not wait for sundown to begin his trip. Surely God would forgive him for travelling on the Sabbath. He would go to shul extra days to make up for this defiance.

Jacob's hands were trembling as he packed his valise and put it in the car. He had never taken a road trip this long before and needed to make certain to take the directions.

Many of the roads were freshly paved, which made the ride a lot smoother than he envisioned. He planned on six hours for the trip to New York and would stop for Petro and a sandwich halfway in. Part of this was so surreal. It had been years since he last saw Elizabeth, and the anticipation clouded his memory. Of one thing he was certain: She was the kindest person he had ever met. He was drawn to her from the first moment he saw her, and she had never been far from his thoughts.

Jacob had experienced a lot in his life but was still inexperienced when it came to affairs of the heart. He hardly understood the feelings racing through him. He just knew that he had never met a woman like Elizabeth before or since and she was never far from his mind.

The trip seemed endless, but as soon as the roads widened, the countryside turned to bright lights, and he knew he was close. Ahead was New York City, and even though he had been there before, he never saw it like this. The buildings were larger and the sidewalks congested. There was an electricity in the air, and he knew he would not be able to sleep a wink tonight.

Jacob paid close attention to the details in his directions and finally found his way to the rooming house Elizabeth had suggested. He parked the car, took out his belongings, and headed for the entrance.

As Jacob walked through the door, he was greeted by a friendly face behind the counter.

"How may I help you?" the man asked.

He appeared to be not much older than Jacob and had a broad smile and twinkle in his eye. Immediately, Jacob relaxed and felt at home.

"My name is Jacob Kalinsky, and I have a room reserved for tonight."

"Yes, of course, Mr. Kalinsky. We have been expecting you. My name is Shlomo, and I will show you to your room."

Ah, Jacob thought. *A clansman.*

Jacob did not realize at this point that he was already in the Lower East Side of New York that housed the major Jewish population in the city.

"Jacob, if you are hungry, I can direct you to a good cafeteria where you can get a hearty meal. Whatever you need, please ask."

Jacob could not have felt better. All his uneasiness of being in a strange place, let alone the circumstances surrounding his being there, diminished.

"Shlomo, thank you, but I have had a long trip and would like to rest."

Shlomo showed Jacob to his room. It was far from extravagant but was warm and inviting.

As soon as Jacob's head hit the pillow, he was sound asleep.

Chapter 21

The Meeting

J. Russ International Appetizers on East Houston Street was where Jacob was to meet Elizabeth. It was a kosher delicatessen run by a Jewish immigrant who also immigrated to America. Although the name did not make one think of shmaltz herring or smoked salmon, the reputation proceeded it. Joel Russ had come from Strzyżów, a small shtetl in Poland. The restaurant had the reputation of having the best food around.

Jacob really did not care about what he was about to eat. He had his heart and mind set solely on seeing Elizabeth for the first time in years. Of course, he arrived early and found a table with a seat facing the door.

Jacob was not a handsome man. He was on the short side, with a bulbous nose; however, he was a pleasant-looking man and kept himself well-groomed. There was certainly no shortage of women in the West End of Boston who had their eyes on him. All that mattered to him now was what would Elizabeth think.

At precisely 9:00 a.m., the door opened, and Jacob and Elizabeth locked eyes. He almost tripped getting up from his seat and ran to her, embracing her in a long-anticipated hug. This was extremely forward for this time, but emotions were running havoc.

"Hello, Jacob. It is so good to see you again."

Jacob could barely speak. Elizabeth was even more beautiful than Jacob remembered. As he led her to her seat, he breathed a long sigh of relief. Her voice was soft and melodic. All he could think of was that he was still a poor chicken farmer's son from a small town in East Europe and she a beautiful Americanized and educated woman. Who could explain affairs of the heart?

"Elizabeth, how have you been?"

It had been six years and many experiences since they last saw each other, and so much was not known.

"Jacob, I have thought about you so much over the years. I always wondered how things would turn out after seeing your father."

The next two hours flew by as Jacob related what had been going on the past several years. Elizabeth listened intently. When Elizabeth spoke, she let Jacob know what had been going on in her life as well.

After Jacob left Ellis Island, Elizabeth contracted tuberculosis. She spent the next several months in the hospital in tenuous situations. She would get better and then go downhill. There were many instances where she thought she was not going to make it. During her worst times, her thoughts always went to Jacob. She always regretted not getting more information on where he was going after he left. It was obvious that Jacob's feelings for her were reciprocal.

When the worst was finally over and Elizabeth had recovered, she completed her nursing studies and has been working in a hospital care unit ever since. The tuberculosis left her lungs weak, and she was prone to respiratory illness but managed to stay on top of it. Through it all, Jacob was never far from her mind, and although she had many opportunities, she never found interest in other men.

Chapter 22

Elizabeth

Elizabeth Levy had been born in America in 1903. Her parents had immigrated to America the year before she was born. They were a very loving couple, and Elizabeth, whom they doted on, was their only child.

Her parents always wanted to give Elizabeth a sister or brother, but it just never happened. Most of their family had been left behind in a small Polish shtetl, but the hope was that the rest of the family would come over as soon as they had the money to do so. Elizabeth's parents became ensconced in the American way of life and settled in the Lower East Side of Manhattan. Her mother was a homemaker, and her father taught Russian history in the community college.

Little by little, more of the family was able to come over and settle in adjoining neighborhoods. Although Elizabeth was an only child, she had many cousins to play with and never felt alone. When Elizabeth was fourteen years old, she noticed a change in her mother: She appeared to disappear in front of Elizabeth's eyes.

"Momma," she would ask, "are you not well?"

Her mother would always smile and respond with a wave of her hand, "No, *mamala*, I am just tired. Do not be concerned."

Of course, concern would be the least of Elizabeth's emotions. By the time she turned fifteen, her mother became very weak to the point that she could no longer get out of bed. Weeks turned into months, and eventually, tuberculosis took the life of Elizabeth's mother.

Elizabeth was inconsolable. She threw herself into her studies and separated herself from the rest of her family. No one could imagine the grief she was feeling. Her mother was her best friend and confidant. How could she get along without her?

Little by little, the grief diminished, and Elizabeth decided that she would dedicate her life to taking care of the sick and needy. She entered nursing school at the young age of sixteen and that following summer volunteered at Ellis Island. Elizabeth had a very caring nature and an abundance of compassion for these poor people coming off the boats. She was kindhearted and gentle to all.

It was the summer of 1920, and a young man by the name of Jacob Kalinsky had just arrived. He seemed so alone and frightened. She immediately took to him and comforted him. He was in quarantine with suspicion of trachoma and tuberculosis. Either condition would have sent him back.

Trachoma was an infectious disease of the eye that could cause blindness. Very often, it was confused with a mild case of conjunctivitis in the immigrants coming over. This misdiagnosis unnecessarily sent many poor immigrants back to where they came from. Fortunately for Jacob, it was soon determined that he did not have tuberculosis. Shortly after, his diagnosis of trachoma was also discarded. He had an eye infection that was treated and eventually cleared up. However, these two questionable diagnoses kept him in quarantine for many weeks on Ellis Island.

Elizabeth managed to spend as much time with him as she could. There was something about this young man that drew her in. He was not especially handsome, but there was something she found very alluring. He was soft-spoken and gentle and seemed to invade her heart. She began to look forward to seeing him every day. She never contemplated that eventually he would be leaving. Every day, she would sit by his bed and discuss just about anything.

Jacob did not speak English, but Elizabeth spoke Yiddish. With this commonality, they were able to converse, and Elizabeth taught Jacob as much English as time allowed.

They commiserated on the fact that both had lost their mothers at very young ages. Of course, Elizabeth could only listen and found it hard to understand what happened to Jacob after his mother's death. Elizabeth had a very kind, loving, and nurturing father who supported her in every way. It was inconceivable to her that a father could just abandon a child the way that Max did.

The days turned into weeks, and eventually, it was time for Jacob to leave. It was unlikely that they would ever see each other again, but Elizabeth gave Jacob her contact information. Jacob had no contact information at that point to exchange. It was an emotional time for both of them, but there was no way of knowing what the future could possibly bring for these two. After all, Jacob was no more than a poor chicken farmer's son from Poland, and Elizabeth was an educated American girl. Affairs of the heart could be fleeting.

After Jacob left, Elizabeth poured herself into taking care of these poor immigrants coming over from Eastern Europe, but her thoughts were never far from Jacob. In the fall, she was to go back to complete her studies in nursing school.

No one could have predicted how sick she would become. By the end of August, her breathing became shallow and she became very weak. She moved off the island and went home to her father and was cared for, in isolation, by her aunts. She had contracted tuberculosis and for the next year was intermittently sick and sometimes at death's door. At these times, she would lie in bed, and her mind would wander to thoughts of Jacob. Where was he? Would she ever see him again? Would she survive this horrible disease? How could she ever return to school?

When the worst was finally over and Elizabeth had recovered, she completed her nursing studies. She threw herself into a job at the Good Presbyterian Hospital in New York. The tuberculosis left her lungs weak, and she was prone to respiratory illness but managed to stay on top of it. Through it all, Jacob was never far from her thoughts, and although she had many opportunities, she never found interest in other men.

She worked day and night and would come home exhausted. This left little time for socializing. From time to time, her mind would go back to the day that Jacob left, and she wondered how she could contact him. Looking for Jacob would have been near impossible. So many names were changed coming off the island, and she had no idea where he would end up. So many people leaving Ellis Island had their names changed. She didn't know how she could possibly find him. All she knew was that he was somewhere in Massachusetts. Also, by now, he had surely forgotten her.

It was at this time, while that thought was in her mind, that a letter arrived. It was from Jacob! Her heart beat so loud and so fast that at first it was difficult to contemplate what this could be about. She slowly opened the letter, and her heart soared. He had not forgotten her.

Now she was sitting across him at the restaurant, and there was no disappointment. She had not felt this kind of happiness in years. It was obvious that the feeling was reciprocal.

Chapter 23

The Nickel Empire

Time flew by, and breakfast came to an end. They still had the whole day ahead of them, and Elizabeth had it planned out. Jacob had never really seen New York other than from the island and train station. Elizabeth wanted to give him a happy memory.

For a nickel, they could take the train to Coney Island. By this time, the subway system in New York City was complete, and it only cost a nickel to get there. Because of this, Coney Island was referred to as the Nickel Empire.

Jacob had never seen an amusement park before, let alone actually been to one. Riding the New York subway was also a new experience for him. This was turning out to be a very exciting day. He had never known this kind of happiness.

Elizabeth was a wonderful tour guide. They boarded the underground train and headed for the seaside resort of Coney Island. What a thrill! All of a sudden, a burst of light came through the windows, and the train emerged from the subway underground. Now they were elevated over a boardwalk, and looking down, Jacob saw throngs of people and could not wait to join them.

Elizabeth took Jacob's arm and led him down the stairs to the boardwalk. Beyond the boardwalk was the ocean and people on the beach. This place shouted *life*, and Jacob could not wait to be part of it.

Jacob felt so comfortable walking arm and arm with Elizabeth. There was no question that the attraction was reciprocal. They walked the boardwalk, eyeing everything around them. The sights and smells were so new and so fresh. Jacob could hardly contain himself. Every vendor offered a new experience for him.

The most astonishing thing of all was Luna's Mile Sky Chaser. He had never seen a roller coaster before, and this one had a drop of eighty feet and the length of the entire park on three sides. Jacob was speechless.

They walked and talked for nearly three hours, stopping only to eat a Nathan's hot dog with all the works. At a nickel apiece, it was considered quite a bargain. A couple of times, they stopped to watch games of chance that could possibly win them a prize. Jacob was too insecure to try his hand at any of these vendor booths for fear of feeling foolish in front of Elizabeth. He somehow knew, however, that he would be back to ride the roller coaster and partake of everything the park had to offer. This time, though, was for attention to Elizabeth. She was even lovelier than he remembered.

The afternoon flew by, and before they knew it, it was time for Jacob to leave. He had a long ride home, and they both had to work early the next morning. Saying goodbye was nearly impossible, but with a hug and a quick peck on the cheek, Jacob promised to call the next day. He just had one more stop to make before he began his journey.

Jacob pulled up to the rooming house and left the car on feet that barely touched the ground. He quickly ran in and approached Shlomo with a request for a reservation two weeks from now. He would return to see Elizabeth and do what he could to make it a special occasion.

"Where," he began, "can I take a woman for a day of dining and entertainment? I am not familiar with the city and want it to be special."

Shlomo could not help but beam at the person whom he had just met a day before. He saw something very special in this young man and wanted to do anything he could to make him happy. He had felt from the onset that he and Jacob would be seeing more of each other, and was happy that this was true.

"Let me put my thinking cap on, make some calls, and get back to you—that is, if you trust me to do so."

"Of course," Jacob replied. "Who could I trust more?"

This was indeed an odd statement coming from someone he had just met, but Jacob had a certain feeling about Shlomo.

As he began to leave, Jacob called out one more request. "Shlomo, you have helped make this the best weekend of my life. I will gladly pay you to send the most beautiful arrangement of flowers to a very special lady. If you can take care of this for me, I will be eternally grateful. Please add on your commission, and let me know how much I owe you. Payment will be sent instantly."

"Jacob, it will be my honor to do this for you."

With pen and paper, Jacob jotted down Elizabeth's address and phone number, along with his own. He had never felt such joy.

Chapter 24

The Rescue

Jacob knew it was getting late to be on the road, but he paid no mind. He was so happy to be able to drive alone with his thoughts of the day. There was no hesitation or disappointment. Elizabeth returned his feelings, and he would return in two weeks' time to be with her again. In the meantime, they could write and talk by phone. All the bad stuff was in his past, and he could finally take joy in the present.

Heschel! Jacob had not even given Heschel a thought while he was away. How did he deal with Max? Although Jacob could care less about Max, he loved Heschel dearly and did not want to create an uneasy situation for him. How did he explain to Max Jacob's absence from his weekly visit? If going to New York was to become a constant thing, and Jacob hoped it would, Max would want explanations. Clearly, he did not deserve the time of day, but Heschel did not deserve to get an increase in his rage because of him. Suddenly, Jacob could not wait to get home and tell Heschel everything about his weekend and find out what Max had said.

The road ahead was dark, and he had hours to go. Jacob saw a small diner up ahead and decided to fuel up on Petro and coffee. As he approached the diner, an uneasy feeling swept over him. He couldn't explain it, but he entered the diner with trepidation. There seemed to be no one around.

"Hello?" he called out. "Is anyone here?"

The diner seemed to be abandoned, and Jacob began to leave. As he was about to reach the door, he heard a slight muffled sound.

It was coming from the back room. His heart was beating out of his body, but he forced himself to inspect, anyway.

He gingerly opened the door to the kitchen and found two people bound and gagged. At first, Jacob froze in place and then quickly took off the gags and untied the owner and his daughter.

"Thank you, thank you," the owner cried.

As soon as he was untied, he ran to the front door and locked it. He then called the police.

Bewildered as he was, Jacob was still shaking from head to toe. *What have I come upon?*

Louis, the owner, began to explain. "My daughter, Rachel, was serving these two men coffee and cake when suddenly they turned on her."

"Empty the cash register!" the larger man yelled out.

It took a minute for Louis and Rachel to see the pistol in this man's hand. Riddled with fear, they did what was demanded. As Rachel emptied the cash register, the other patron dragged Louis in back and tied his hands and feet and gagged him. All Louis could think about was his poor daughter out in front with them. What would they do to her?

Before long, the larger man dragged Rachel to the back as well and bound her the same way.

"Do not make a sound or try to get free for at least an hour," he said menacingly.

They then grabbed the cash, whatever food they could jam into a bag, and left.

The time seemed to drag by until Jacob appeared. Louis could not believe his good fortune that these men hurt neither him nor his daughter.

"Please, what can I ever do to repay you?" asked Louis.

Jacob looked stunned that he had come across this situation at this time in his life, when all he wanted to do was drive home and think of Elizabeth. "What is your name?"

"I am Louis Soloman, and this is my daughter, Rachel. Nothing like this has ever happened to us before. We have been running this diner for the past ten years without incident. We have no way of knowing if these crooks are going to come back and do more harm."

Finally, when Louis stopped rambling, Jacob was able to introduce himself. "I am Jacob Kalinsky from Boston. I was on my way home from New York and thought I would stop for fuel for my car and coffee for myself. I am happy I was able to be of help."

All of a sudden, the sound of a siren was approaching. Louis explained to the police what had just occurred. They took down statements from all three and took Jacob's contact information in case they needed to reach him for comment later.

After the police left, Jacob was spent. It was getting late, and he still had a long drive ahead of him. Louis insisted on filling up his gas tank and loaded him up with sandwiches and a thermos of hot coffee. Jacob let Louis know that he would be coming back this way again in two weeks' time and would stop by to check on him and Rachel.

In the meantime, Jacob could not wait to get back on the road and be alone with his thoughts of Elizabeth. The past hour had been surreal, and he just wanted to shake it out of his mind.

Chapter 25

The Homecoming

It was midnight when Jacob finally walked through the door. Certain that Heschel would be asleep, he decided to not wake him. That thought was short-lived.

"Heschel, Heschel, wake up. I have so much to tell you."

Bleary-eyed, Heschel was suddenly alert.

"First, I must tell you about Elizabeth."

As Jacob regaled Heschel with his experiences of the past twenty-four hours, Heschel kept thinking to himself that this was not the same person he had last seen a little over a day ago. There was a lightness that had never been there before. As amused as Heschel was over Jacob's excitement, he was also very happy for him.

Then Jacob told him about Louis and Rachel and the gas station-diner robbery. Wow! As long as everyone came out fine, it was a great story.

Later in life, when people spoke of Jacob, it was always about the story. He could find delight in almost anything as long as he got a story out of it.

Finally, they were both exhausted, but it was almost time to get up and go to work. They downed pots full of coffee and managed to stay awake while Heschel told Jacob about his experiences of the past day with Max and Esther.

It was always expected that Jacob and Heschel would make the trip to Millis every Sunday to spend the afternoon at Max's home with Esther and little David. Even though they considered themselves grown men and did not enjoy these visits, Jacob and Heschel felt compelled to make this trip every week.

When Heschel told Max why Jacob was absent, his temper flared. Max had suffered from diabetes and eventually had a leg amputated due to that disease. Because of this, he was confined to a wheelchair and counted on the boys' help on Sundays. He was certainly not deserving of this kind of loyalty, but time had done nothing to calm the anger that was inherent to him. Jacob did not want to put the onus of visiting Max on Heschel alone, but he now had a life, and if Heschel was smart, he, too would get one. Max had never been much of a father to them, so why should they be such good sons to him?

Both boys were beyond exhaustion, and the matter regarding Max and Jacob would have to wait for another day. Jacob did not want to get off the high he had been on since leaving New York. He would work out a remedy that would never be agreeable to Max, but for that matter, such a thing did not exist. He owed Max nothing. Esther was too consumed with her son, David, to really care about either boy. She was as evil as Max and as self-consumed to really be a solution to anything.

Both boys finally got dressed and headed off to work. They were both accomplished furniture makers by now with an outstanding reputation. Jacob continued his studies independently on climate and its effects on tangible materials. As time went by, he gained much respect from his neighborhood of patrons and suppliers. Now with the prospect of Elizabeth, he felt life was almost complete, and he was not going to allow negativity to invade.

That evening, he called Elizabeth as promised. Hearing her voice only secured the feeling he was having. She had received the flowers that Shlomo had promised to send and was overwhelmed.

"Jacob, this was so extravagant. The flowers are beautiful, and the sentiment even more so. You have brought so much sunshine into my life."

He was falling hard. Jacob had never been in a relationship before, and this just seemed so natural. It was a long-distance call, and the charge was running up, but he hated to hang up. He promised to call again at the end of the week and would return in two weeks' time.

"I have a very special day planned for us when I return."

As soon as he hung up from Elizabeth, he called Shlomo. "Thank you so much for sending the flowers for me. Elizabeth was overjoyed with the presentation. Please tell me what I owe you and will telegraph the money to you immediately."

Shlomo then proceeded to explain to Jacob the plans he had in mind for his return trip to New York City. Jacob could not believe his ears when he heard what Shlomo had put together for him. Money would be no object. Jacob made a good weeks' pay and spent very little. He knew that he had little time to actually be with Elizabeth on these visits, so he wanted to make every minute count. The next two weeks would drag on without mercy.

Jacob dreaded the inevitable confrontation with his father. He definitely wanted to come from a position of strength and not weakness. For Jacob, this would be difficult because Max had always been a tyrant and had not one iota of softness or compassion in him. Losing his leg made him even meaner.

Jacob worked very hard during the first week he was home from New York. He tried to put his mind on work and nothing else, although Elizabeth kept creeping into his thoughts.

Finally, Sunday rolled around, and Jacob and Heschel made the obligatory visit to Millis. As soon as they entered the house, Jacob could feel his father's wrath.

"Oh, so you decided to return from your weekend of running around with a hussy from New York City. Well, now that you have that out of your system, you can get back to your normal routine. Esther is gathering eggs in the henhouse and could use a hand. Both you boys go see what you can do to help her."

Heschel immediately stood up to go but was instantly pushed back down by Jacob.

"Papa, we may be your sons, but you have never been a father to us," Jacob said. "We are now grown men and have worked hard to achieve whatever success we have, no thanks to you. We work hard all week, and Sunday is the only day we have for ourselves. Do not expect us to drive out here every week to be instructed by you to do your bidding. If you need help around the farm, hire it. It will more than pay for itself. We have both paid our dues for being born to you, but no more. I have met a kind and compassionate woman who has shown me more kindness in the short time I have known her than you have in my lifetime."

Where was this strength coming from? Heschel wondered. He had never seen this side of Jacob. Little did he know that at just that moment, Jacob was wondering the same thing. He had reached his saturation level, and all the vitriol that he had endured his whole life came spewing out of him and back at the culprit who created it.

Stunned, Max lifted up the iron cane that never left his side and screamed for his ungrateful son to get out of his house. At that moment, Esther and little David came in the door. David was very timid and small for his age, but when he saw Heschel and Jacob, he beamed.

Esther surveyed the scene in front of her and grabbed David up and took him outside. She was just as mean-spirited as Max and was not going to let the one thing in her life that meant anything to her at all be subjected to this fighting. Confused, David began to cry.

Jacob did not want to hurt the boy but was put between a rock and a hard place. David would always be number one in Esther's life, and as close as anyone could be, he would be number one to Max's as well. It was just then that Jacob made up his mind to cut his father and stepmother out of his life, even if it meant never seeing David again either.

Jacob grabbed Heschel and ran out the door. "Heschel, we are now free of this horrible person. I am never going back, and I suggest you do the same. Nothing good is ever going to come of us having a relationship with this man and his wife. From this moment on, we have to shape our own futures and ensure that they be as happy and filled with love as they can be. Are you with me on this?"

Heschel was speechless.

They both got in the car with a lightness that was not there before. They were brought up, mostly by Jordanna, to be respectful of their elders, but this had gone too far. Max had no love for these boys, and he certainly did nothing to earn their respect or gratitude. After all, there had been nothing to be grateful for.

The ride back to Boston was almost gleeful. How dare Max suggest that Elizabeth was a hussy? Heschel was slightly less happy. It had all happened so fast, and he hadn't had time to digest the fallout from what just went down. Jacob was more pragmatic but understood Heschel's dilemma. This was, after all, his father. There was no love there, but there would always be a familial connection.

Jacob would never forget the hell he endured as a result of his father sending him away. To this day, Heschel was never told of that awful night at the brothel when Jacob lost all his innocence. To this day, no one knew. At times, Jacob would withdraw into himself and be very pensive. At these times, Heschel would ask out of concern, "Jacob, what is it? Can you share with me the pain that often overtakes you?"

"No matter, Heschel. Sometimes I just reflect on our lives and wonder what road we might have travelled had Mama not died so young."

Heschel hoped that now that Jacob had found Elizabeth again, there would be fewer maudlin moments.

By the time they reached Boston, Heschel began to relax a bit more. As much as he disliked his father and really despised Esther, he decided to take their coming absences on a day-by-day basis. After all, he always had the option of going back to see them, although he was pretty sure that wouldn't happen.

Chapter 26

The Next Chapter

Jacob spent the next week throwing himself into his work. After several conversations with Shlomo, the plan was to take Elizabeth to the *Ziegfeld Follies* matinee and then out for an early dinner before heading back to Boston.

Shlomo secured the tickets for Jacob. He had never been to a professional play, let alone a Broadway spectacular. He told Shlomo to get the best seats possible and to spare no cost. It wasn't as if Jacob had splurged on anything in his life up until now. In the morning, he would meet Elizabeth and just walk around Manhattan until it was time to go to the theater.

All he knew about the *Ziegfeld Follies* was that it was a lavish review of vaudeville and musical variety. It featured beautiful, somewhat lightly clad women. Elizabeth had no idea of where they were going; he had just told her that it would be special.

Once again, Saturday came, and Jacob headed out for New York City. Although he could barely contain himself at the thought of seeing Elizabeth again, he was not as nervous as he was before. He knew he would be well-received. He phoned Elizabeth twice during the week, and they planned to meet up at the same place as before, have a light breakfast, and go on from there.

Saturday evening, he pulled up to the familiar rooming house and was warmly greeted by Shlomo. They felt like old friends by now. Jacob brought him a fine bottle of whiskey, and they both sat back and toasted their new friendship. Shlomo learned much of Jacob's past that night, and it was then that they developed a tight bond.

Sometimes, old souls come together easily, and these two felt the kinship immediately. Shlomo felt as though he had been let in to a special place, having set up the plans for Jacob's visit, and could not wait to hear about the outcome.

Jacob could not believe how comfortable he felt opening up to Shlomo. He tended to be a very private person, but Elizabeth had an effect on him that brought out a different personality. He felt lighter and not at all threatened to open up to this man who was actually a complete stranger. No matter, it brought out the best in him, and he was happy.

The two men did a very good job working on the whiskey, and finally, Jacob bid Shlomo good night and headed off to bed. As excited as he was about the following day, he would sleep soundly, thanks to the heavy drinking that he was not accustomed to.

Sunday morning finally came around, and Jacob's heart was pounding. He raced down the stairs to find a hungover Shlomo sitting at the desk.

"Shlomo," said Jacob. "I drank just as much as you but clearly have not had the same effect."

"Perhaps being in love covers your cells with a protective gear," said Shlomo.

Being in love? Jacob knew that he was feeling something foreign, but was it love? He was so inexperienced at affairs of the heart. Shlomo, however, saw right through him.

"Jacob, here are your tickets to the show. Make sure to get there early, and prepare to be amazed. The tickets were not cheap, but you will see that it was money well-spent."

At $2.50 a ticket, plus a $5.00 cover charge, it was the most money Jacob had ever spent for his entertainment. Of course, the seats were the best and close to the stage. When it came to Elizabeth, money was of no concern. Her smile would be worth every dime. An extravagant dinner would have to wait for another time. After the theater, he planned to walk to Horn and Hardart. This in itself would be an adventure for him because he had never been to an automat before.

"Shlomo, I will be back before I leave for Boston to fill you in on today's events." Jacob had never had a friend to confide in before. He always had Heschel, but that relationship was different. He always felt protective of his younger brother.

Jacob got to the diner and was surprised to find that Elizabeth was already there waiting for him. He was elated.

"Am I late?" he asked.

"No, no," she replied. "I was up early and thought I would walk down and be here when you arrived."

Jacob was elated. They ordered coffee and muffins and spent the next hour totally engulfed in conversation. This was a new and improved Jacob. He felt so comfortable with her.

"Elizabeth, I have so looked forward to seeing you again. I have a wonderful day planned, but we have a few hours to spare. I thought we might take the subway to the area that has all the theaters and just walk around until the show I am taking you to begins."

"Jacob, you have tickets to a theater? Even though I live here, I have never been to a live performance."

Smiling, Jacob responded, "Then we will experience this first-time event together."

He was not going to tell her just yet which theater they would be going to. Even he understood the extreme nature of his choice. Seeing the *Ziegfeld Follies* would be a unique experience for most anyone.

They took the subway to Times Square, and when they walked out of the train station, the sun was shining so brightly. It was a perfect midsummer day. Jacob was totally overcome with emotion at the sight of all the hustle and bustle of people. It was late morning on a Sunday, and he had never seen so many automobiles in one place before. The women were lavishly dressed and the men all wearing suits with cravats. He really felt underdressed, but Elizabeth kept reassuring him that he was fine.

They walked through Times Square and looked in all the shop windows. Boston was certainly not a hick town by any means, but New York City seemed to be a country all its own.

"Elizabeth, there is so much to take in here. How can anyone keep anything straight? I just want to keep turning my head this way and that and listen to all the sounds of people and cars. How do you keep from getting lost?"

"Jacob, I have grown up here, and although much of this progress is new, it was gradual to me. This is the only life I've known. Sometimes, I long for a quiet countryside."

They kept walking up and down the streets, still arm in arm. Even the smaller side streets were lined with shops and boutiques.

All of a sudden, Jacob saw a shop with a sign hanging over it that read "Frank's Furniture Restoration."

"Elizabeth, this shop seems to be open. I see a man working inside and would love to go in and speak to him."

"Of course, Jacob. I too would be interested to see what he is doing."

Jacob opened the door to the shop and introduced himself and Elizabeth to whom he presumed to be Frank. "Hello, I am a visitor to this city, but I think you and I have much in common. I also have a shop in Boston that does furniture restoration and repair. I was wondering if I could see what you are doing."

Frank had a warm demeanor, and quickly shook Jacob's hand. "I am Frank Stevens, and this is my shop. I normally do not work on Sundays, but people will soon be coming back from the shore, and I am overwhelmed with work."

"Well," said Jacob, "I certainly won't take up much of your time, but I haven't come across many people that I consider artisans in this field, and judging by what I am seeing, you certainly are an artisan. I consider myself to do quality work as well but am always interested in learning from more experienced people than me. I will be coming to this city frequently and wonder if I might drop in to visit from time to time."

"Jacob," said Frank, "if you're at all interested, I'd be happy to hand you some tools and see what you can do. I have been short-handed since my last employee left to go back to the old country. It's difficult to find anyone who has the same work ethic as myself."

Suddenly, Jacob was hit with a thunderbolt. Heschel was still running the shop with him back at home.

What if, he thought, *I split my time between Boston and New York? I could work part-time for Frank, make enough money to rent a room, see more of Elizabeth, and not have to drive out on Saturday nights and drive back on Sunday evenings.*

Of course, he would first have to run this by Elizabeth and make certain that she was on the same page emotionally as he was. Then again, it wasn't as though Frank was offering him a job yet.

"Frank, until what time do you think you will be in the shop?"

"Well," he replied, "at the rate I'm going, I will be here way past dinner."

"We are going to a matinee performance at the theater. Would it be all right if I stopped in when we got out? I may have something to discuss with you."

"Certainly," said Frank. "I'll look forward to seeing you again."

As soon as Jacob and Elizabeth left the shop, Elizabeth could hardly contain herself. "Jacob, what was that all about?"

At the end of the street, there was a small park, and Jacob led her over to a bench so they could speak.

"Elizabeth, you are constantly on my mind, and seeing you every other week for less than twenty-four hours is not what I want. I want to see more of you and see where this takes us. I cannot give up the business I am building in Boston, but if I worked for Frank part-time, I would make enough money to rent a room and court you properly.

"I could be in Boston half the time and in this city the other half. Heschel would still be running the shop in Boston. I would do this only if it was something you wanted as well. I hope I'm not being presumptuous. Think about it, and if this plan intrigues you as well, then I will approach Frank after the theater and see if he's interested in hiring me on a part-time basis."

Jacob was a firm believer that things happened for a reason. It was *bashert* that he happened to be walking down this particular street at this particular time. Things just seemed to be falling in place, and he couldn't be happier.

It was now time to get to the theater. Both of them were practically giddy at the events of the day. As they approached the New Amsterdam Theater, Elizabeth grinned from ear to ear. She had certainly heard of the famous Florenz Ziegfeld but could not even fathom attending one of his shows. As they entered the theater to take their seats, she squeezed Jacob's hand extra hard and looked up at him lovingly. No one had ever treated her with this much generosity and consideration. Yes, she was falling in love right behind Jacob.

Soon the theater filled with happy patrons. Elizabeth wanted to take in every sight and sound. She would never forget this day. This particular review was not one of Ziegfeld's finest and got terrible reviews, but with them never having been to an extravagant theater performance of any kind before, it didn't really matter to either of them. It didn't help the reviews that the assistant director dropped dead on opening night either. The show was riddled with bad luck from day 1. If only the electricity coming from Elizabeth and Jacob could have been felt throughout the theater.

All of a sudden, there was a quiet hush throughout the audience as the lights dimmed and the curtain went up. They were about to see a lavish review called *No Foolin'*. It could have been called chopped liver for all these two cared. They were mesmerized at the costumes and the variety acts, but mostly, they were mesmerized with each other.

Once the show was over, Elizabeth and Jacob walked back to Frank's Furniture Restoration. They were greeted with a bounding "Hello." Jacob could not mistake this for anything but encouragement. Working part-time for Frank would allow him to spend more time with Elizabeth and make more money on the side to pay for his keep in New York.

He wasn't quite sure how Heschel would feel about this, but when he saw how happy Jacob was, he hoped he would be happy as well. Also, Heschel was getting an interest in socializing and had taken several women out for lunch. This was recent, and Jacob would glow inside at the tales that Heschel would relate. Perhaps he would find the one while Jacob spent time in New York. Yes, life was turning out pretty good.

Frank sat him down and made him an offer. Jacob would have taken peanuts to make this arrangement work; however, Frank made him such a generous offer that Jacob almost fell out of his seat. He would work for Frank Thursdays, Fridays, and Sundays. He would go back to Boston on Sunday nights and work Monday through Wednesday. The adrenaline was so high that the thought of being exhausted did not even enter Jacob's mind.

Elizabeth sat by quietly while the men negotiated their understanding, not that there was actually any negotiating.

As Elizabeth and Jacob left the shop, Jacob could not hide his excitement.

"Elizabeth, this opportunity is amazing. I can't believe how we stumbled upon this. The arrangement works as well for Frank as it does for me. His wife has been complaining about how much time he spends in the shop, and now he'll be able to be home more. I, of course, am most excited at the prospect of being able to see you more and give you a proper courtship. I haven't even asked if this is all right with you. If seeing more of me is not what you want, please tell me now. I guess I have taken so much for granted, thinking you feel the same about me as I do you."

"Jacob, I couldn't be happier. You are on my mind constantly, and I look forward to being able to see more of you. When you are here, you will come to my aunt's home for Shabbos dinner. You will love my family."

Jacob had not had a real Shabbos dinner since he lost his mother. The thought of having a real family to spend time with filled him with emotion. Yes, this was going to work.

The walk to Horn and Hardart was short. Jacob had never been to an automat before. Horn and Hardart was an innovative concept in dining. The automat was already in wide use in Europe but was slower for Americans to accept. The food was fresh and cheap, but the concept of putting a nickel or a dime into a slot and taking out your food of choice from behind a glass door was a little strange. Once one got the concept, it became a fun game.

Every section was labeled according to whether it was salads, entrées, or desserts. They were mostly famous for their mac and cheese. The staff would quickly fill the spaces as they emptied so that the food was always fresh. Their place was behind the glass doors, so they could see what was needed and refill it. They would also give change with lightning speed to customers who needed it. Nothing like this was seen in Boston—yet.

Horn and Hardart was also famous for their coffee. It was dispensed from silver dolphin spouts that came from Italy. It was thought to be the best coffee in New York.

This was truly a fabulous day for both Jacob and Elizabeth. They lingered over dinner, and the conversation came as easy as ever. Soon, it was time for Jacob to head back to Boston. This time, he walked Elizabeth to the train station with the idea that he would be returning in two weeks to find a place to stay and be back every week after that. He would be coming in on Thursday and would have his first Shabbos dinner with Elizabeth and her family on Friday night. He was on cloud nine.

It was difficult for Jacob to tear himself away from Elizabeth this time. A hug would not do. He gently put his arms around her and gave her a long, gentle kiss. Although he had not had much experience in the world of romance, this came so naturally to both of them. Elizabeth kissed him back with as much emotion.

As difficult as it was to leave Elizabeth again, he soothed himself with the fact that the next time would be longer. He watched her walk away until she was out of sight and then left to say goodbye to Shlomo.

As soon as he got back to Shlomo's rooming house, Shlomo witnessed a beaming man whose feet were barely touching the ground. Jacob related the events of the day.

When he heard that Jacob wanted to find a room to rent for the times he would be working for Frank, he exclaimed with much excitement, "Why would you go elsewhere when you have a perfectly good place to stay right here? I will give you a great discount for being a semi-permanent guest, and you can leave your car here and take the train into the city. Also, rent in Manhattan will be so much higher."

Jacob could not believe his good fortune. Shlomo was almost like another brother to him. "Of course. Why didn't this occur to me in the first place?"

The time was getting late, and Jacob still wanted to stop in Connecticut to check in on Louis and Rachel. He recounted to Shlomo the events from the last time he had travelled home from the city. He had promised to check in on them the next time he travelled. Besides, it was the perfect opportunity to stop for petro.

Chapter 27

On the Road Again

Jacob bid goodbye to his new friend and looked forward to seeing him again. With that, he got in his car and sped off. The first two hours passed so quickly with thoughts of Elizabeth on his mind. They were great thoughts filled with emotion.

Finally, he came to the exit on the road where the gas station and diner were. As he pulled up, he could see Louis coming out to greet him. As soon as Louis recognized him, he was all smiles and grabbed Jacob up in a big bear hug. He credited Jacob with saving his life, although if truth be told, someone would have come along eventually.

"Jacob, my friend, how wonderful to see you again. Rachel is in the diner and would love to make you something to eat."

"Thank you. Nothing to eat, but I would love a cup of coffee. I have a way to go yet and need to stay awake. A cup of very strong coffee would be great."

Jacob entered the diner and saw a very different Rachel from what he had remembered. Of course, he originally had found her bound and terrified. This was a very attractive young woman with an easy smile. Jacob was happy to see that her ordeal had not had a lasting effect on her.

"Hello, Rachel. Do you remember me?"

"Of course, Jacob. How could I ever forget you and what you did for my father and me? How have you been?"

"I think the question should be how have *you* been? I have thought of you and your father often and was looking forward to dropping in on you the next time I traveled from New York. I am so happy to see how well you are doing. That was quite an ordeal you went through. I hope those men did not come back."

"Well, if they had, we would be prepared. Father will never again allow us to be vulnerable." With that, she produced a pistol from under the counter.

"Certainly, you don't want to ever use that thing," said Jacob.

"Well, if it's a question of them or us, I will make the right decision. Now what can I get for you?"

"A very strong, hot cup of coffee would be great."

"A cup of coffee must be accompanied by a slice of my mother's famous apple pie."

The words *apple pie* struck a chord with Jacob. It was the one thing he could never turn down.

As he sipped his coffee and devoured the pie, Rachel told him a little about herself. She had two older brothers who lived in Boston. They were both married with families. Her father had hoped one of them would take over the diner and petro station, but they both had other things in mind. They both finished college and had gone on to become professionals, one an engineer and the other a history teacher.

Rachel stayed behind and helped out with the diner and gas station. She was not upset at the way things turned out. She loved her parents and was happy to be able to take over for them. She lived with them in a house behind the diner and was comfortable with life. She had no interest in furthering her education. She had, in fact, aspirations to be a wife and mother. She had no goals in life other than that.

Jacob found this a little sad. He would have grabbed at any opportunity to further his education. Even now, with thoughts of spending the rest of his life with Elizabeth, he still aspired to educate himself and push himself to be the best he could be.

Soon, Louis came into the diner. "You're all filled up and ready to go."

"Louis, what do I owe you?"

"Sorry, Jacob, your money is no good here. After what you did for us, I can never repay you."

"All right, Louis. However, I will be coming this way every week and will take my business elsewhere if you do not take payment next time."

"And what will be taking you by here so often, Jacob?"

Jacob related bits and pieces of his life and his relationship with Elizabeth. Although he was visibly excited about his turn of events, it was apparent from the look on Rachel's face that she was slightly disappointed. She found Jacob to be a very pleasant-looking man with a kind and generous nature. She was hoping to get to know him better. Her father also liked him very much.

Oh well, she thought. At least she might get a new friend in him, especially if he would be coming by every week.

It was probably at this very moment that Jacob thought of Heschel. Possibly, Rachel and Heschel would make a match. He had so much to relate to Heschel when he got home. It couldn't come fast enough.

Chapter 28

A Man in Love

Once again, Heschel was fast asleep by the time Jacob arrived home. Once again, Jacob could not wait till morning to relate all the news to Heschel. As excited as he was about working part-time for Frank, he would still have to run it by Heschel. If Heschel was not happy about this arrangement, then Jacob would have to find another way. He would never do anything to make Heschel unhappy.

This time, Jacob decided to sleep on things. There was too much to discuss to try to speak with his half-asleep brother. Although Jacob's mind was reeling over the events of the weekend, he quickly fell into a deep slumber.

The following morning, Jacob sat across an excited Heschel. "I cannot wait to hear how your trip went this time."

Jacob first filled Heschel in with his initial meeting with Shlomo and then on to his day with Elizabeth. He related, as best he could, the events of the day regarding *Ziegfeld Follies*, the automat, and then back to Frank's Furniture Restoration.

Initially, Heschel was a bit confused, but as Jacob scoped out the plan, he actually got excited. If the work got to be too much for Heschel alone on the days Jacob was not there, he would hire another worker. Yes, he was beginning to imagine this.

Jacob was overcome with emotion. After all, Heschel was a caring and sensitive man and would never do anything that might hurt Jacob. They were two brothers who could not be closer.

"Heschel, I must also tell you about my meeting with Louis and Rachel. This is the family that owns the diner and gas station in Connecticut. I had promised to look in on them next time I came that way. They could not have been more cordial. Rachel is really a very attractive young woman. I think you would like her."

"Hold on, Jacob. You are getting away from yourself. One thing at a time. I am just beginning to feel comfortable getting out and socializing with the women I know. Let's see how things go with Elizabeth first. Eventually, I will make this trip with you to meet her. Possibly she could come here, and we'll show her Boston. Everything is happening very fast. Let's take it one step at a time."

Normally Jacob would have been the voice of reason, but for once, Heschel was.

The following week seemed to drag by. Jacob reconfirmed Elizabeth's feelings for him by his phone calls. They had to keep them brief because of the long-distance charges, but the content was warm enough to make his heart soar. They were both falling hard for each other. The future that once looked so bleak was looking brighter and brighter.

Jacob poured everything he had into the next week. His shop had become very popular, and the fact that he could make educated recommendations on which fabric would wear the best or which kind of wood finish would last the longest made people trust him. He knew that some fibers would naturally block out the sun and not fade. He knew that some metals would refrain from rusting, and he knew that in the summer most woods would expand and in the colder climates it would contract and possibly crack.

Ever since the molasses flood, he studied up on all these things, and it only made his expertise more valuable. Although nothing was ever bulletproof, his clients knew that his knowledge made his furniture last longer and wear better than most. He, of course, passed everything he learned on to Heschel so that the partnership worked seamlessly. Even though he never made it to college, the education he provided on his own was priceless. Frank would soon find that a jewel in the rough came into his shop one fine day.

The following Thursday, Jacob left work, cleaned up, and once again headed to New York. The ride was more relaxing this time. He knew he would be staying longer, would be seeing a very receptive Elizabeth, and would be starting his new job with Frank. The one big difference in this trip was that he would be meeting Elizabeth's family at her aunt's Shabbos dinner. It had been many years since he celebrated the Sabbath, and even then, it had been with his dear mother, Sarah.

He never stopped thinking of her and how different his life would have been had she lived. He would catch himself and remember that *should have, would have, could have* were phrases that could only be harmful. He always vowed to never think that way but sometimes would lapse into "If only." None of these phrases could be helpful; in fact, they were only hurtful.

It was always important to deal with what is and not what could have been. The past would have to remain the past, and looking forward was the only thing that mattered.

It was this thought that brought a huge smile to Jacob's face. As long as Elizabeth was in his future, he would regret nothing.

Chapter 29

⁓⁂⁓

A New Venture

Jacob arrived at Shlomo's later that evening but was so exhausted that he could barely lift his arm for a brotherly hug and headed straight to bed. All the awkwardness of a new situation was lifted, and he felt right at home.

The following morning, Jacob woke up early, got dressed, and headed for the subway into Manhattan. He knew that Elizabeth would be getting ready for work but would call her later to let her know he had arrived. He definitely was seeing a future newer and brighter than he ever thought possible.

Jacob arrived at Frank's Furniture Restoration with bags of coffee and Danish. Frank was so delighted to see him and insisted they begin their day devouring the goodies that Jacob had brought.

"So tell me, Jacob, are you excited about this new venture in your life?"

Not holding back, Jacob, very forthright, replied, "Frank, as excited as I am about working and learning from you, I am most excited at being able to spend more time with Elizabeth. The relationship may be new, but it took years of yearning to come to this point."

He related to Frank, as well as he could, about his time in Poland, Jordanna, and his meeting with Elizabeth.

Frank had all he could do to hide his amazement. "You have lived more than two lifetimes, my friend. With all you have been through, you manage to smile and show a soft, loving demeanor. How is it that you are not angry and sullen?"

"Frank, I view every success as a positive in my life. When things could have gone one way or the other, and I survived, I think of how lucky I am. I would rather my cup remain half-full than half-empty."

"Jacob, my new and intelligent friend, I think working with you is going to be more of a learning experience for me than for you. However, the day is short, and we have much to do. Show me what you can do."

Frank was astounded at Jacob's knowledge. His workmanship was impeccable. All Frank had to do was point a finger, and Jacob immediately knew the task at hand.

Where did you come from? he wondered.

It had to be divine intervention that brought Jacob into his shop that day.

Customers coming into the shop that first day would ask questions about fabrics and designs for their furniture. Frank was amazed at how knowledgeable Jacob was. He had not known about his interest in more than putting hammer and nail to wood and veneer. Jacob was a walking encyclopedia about everything pertaining to anything about furniture. He soaked up knowledge like a sponge.

At the end of the day, Frank let Jacob know how pleased he was about Jacob's performance. It wasn't only the fact that he was a great technician; he had a wonderful demeanor about him. The customers seemed to love him. He was pleasant and really paid attention when someone was speaking to him. He listened with great interest and looked everyone in the eye. Yes, Jacob had wandered into Frank's shop one day, and Frank wanted to pinch himself at his good fortune.

Jacob wished Frank a good Shabbos, with the understanding that he would be back first thing Sunday morning. He headed back to Shlomo's to wash and change his clothes and then on to pick up Elizabeth. He was very excited to meet her family.

When Jacob arrived at Elizabeth's home, it was just sundown. He was greeted by a very jovial man who introduced himself as Elizabeth's father, Mr. Levy.

"Jacob, I am so very pleased to meet you. Elizabeth has told me so much about you. Has she mentioned that I teach European history at the community college? I fear that I may monopolize your time this evening with questions about your experiences growing up in Eastern Europe."

"Oh, Father," a sweet voice came up from behind. "You're going to frighten him. Hello, Jacob, and Good Shabbos."

Jacob turned around and looked at this beautiful young woman whom he was falling in love with. "Good Shabbos, Elizabeth. It has been many years since I have had the pleasure of joining in a Sabbath welcoming."

"Come, children. We will be late for the family gathering."

As Jacob, Elizabeth, and Mr. Levy left their apartment, Jacob could not get over the easiness he felt with this new experience. Mr. Levy was as warm and accepting as Elizabeth.

They walked two blocks until they reached a similar brownstone. "This is where my aunt Evelyn and uncle Stanley live."

Elizabeth went on to explain that her extended family came to New York shortly after she had been born, and all her cousins, aunts, and uncles spent every Shabbos and every holiday together. They were as close as could be, and no one ever felt alone. They knew they could count on each other through good times and bad. Jacob's relationship with his father was a total enigma to them. This was the kind of family Jacob had always dreamed of having.

Elizabeth's family was very religious but not orthodox. It was acceptable for men and women to sit with each other. With this in mind, Jacob accepted everyone's hugs and handshakes as he came through the door. The huge dining room was set with beautiful dishes and candlesticks. The smells coming from the kitchen were like nothing he had ever experienced. The beautiful homemade challahs adorned the table, and everyone took their places.

Aunt Evelyn covered her head with a lace cloth and lit the Shabbos candles. She drew her hands around the candles and swept them toward her face three times and then shielded her eyes. She then recited the blessing: "Barukh atah Adonai Eloheinu Melekh ha'olam asher kid'shanu b'mitzvotav v'tzinanu l'hadlik ner shel shabbat."

In English, this translates to "Blessed are you, Lord our God, Ruler of the universe who has sanctified us with commandments and commanded us to light Shabbat candles."

The lighting of the candles is required at sundown on Friday nights for the sake of representing harmony in the home as well as welcoming in the Sabbath.

Tears ran down Jacob's face. The last time he was at a Shabbat dinner and heard these words welcoming in the Sabbath was when his beloved mother, Sarah, was alive. It brought back so many memories. His eyes roamed around the table, and he felt the love and the joy that enveloped these people. He prayed that this would be only the beginning of a wonderful tradition that he could also share with Heschel. He reached over and took Elizabeth's hand under the table. They locked eyes, and she totally understood his reaction.

This was followed by an amazing feast of soups and chicken and every and any side dish that he could imagine. Later, after the women cleared the plates, the men sat around and sang beautiful, happy songs. This was truly a night to remember.

When it was time to leave, Aunt Evelyn made him promise to return. She packed him a care package to take back to the rooming house. He had never felt more wanted in his life. He walked Elizabeth and Mr. Levy home and promised to return the following afternoon.

As Mr. Levy walked up the stairs to his apartment, he waved Jacob goodbye and told him how privileged he was to meet him.

He felt privileged? I'm sure that I must have heard wrong, thought Jacob. *The honor is on my side.*

Elizabeth took Jacob's hand, looked him in the eyes, and told him that her father had been so touched by Jacob's life story that he, indeed, felt it was his privilege to meet him.

"Elizabeth, I am so overcome with emotion right now. My own flesh and blood, my own father, would never have thought that about me. I don't even know how to rationalize these feelings. I do, however, know that I have fallen in love with you and hope that your feelings toward me are the same. I know this is happening so fast, but years and miles have come between us, and I don't want to wait forever to let my feelings be known. Your family was so welcoming, and unless I am reading too much into this, they are as happy for you as I am for me."

"Jacob, I barely understand it myself, but there is not one minute of every day that you are not in my thoughts. I love you as well, and am certain that there will never be anyone else for me."

With that, Jacob wrapped his arms around Elizabeth, kissed her, and held her in a long embrace. In 1926, this might have been construed as a very forward move, but the feelings between them were unmistakable. Even so, they would have to slow down a bit. So much was changing so fast.

One last embrace, and Jacob watched as Elizabeth ran up the stairs to her apartment. In the morning, she would attend Shabbat services with her father, and then Jacob would arrive for lunch. After that, nothing mattered as long as they were together.

The following day, Jacob arrived at Elizabeth's home for lunch. She had prepared a wonderful meal, and this gave Mr. Levy a chance to get to know Jacob. Except for that awful, shameful time at Jordanna's, Jacob was an open book. He was open to all questions about his life. He really felt that Elizabeth's father was just showing an interest in his past, not because her father was nosy but because he was really interested. He showed a lot of compassion for Jacob and let him know how much he respected what he had made of his life. So many others could easily have gone in a different direction. He was a teacher of Eastern European history and was getting information firsthand from a true survivor. He truly liked this young man who was courting his daughter.

After lunch, Jacob and Elizabeth walked throughout the Lower East Side of the city. She pointed out the various spots, such as the pickle man who reached into barrels of pickles up to his elbows to fill in containers for his patrons. By the end of the day, there was not a pickle to be had. There was the fish man who served buckets of herring and onions. Yes, the Lower East Side of New York was a mecca for good food. Being the Sabbath and this being primarily a Jewish neighborhood, most of these shops were closed, but for sure, Jacob would be back the next day to partake of these gastronomic delights.

He felt so at home here and could not wait to bring Heschel to meet the family.

That evening, he brought Elizabeth to a local restaurant, where they dined on briskets like he had never tasted. It could have been sawdust. All he had eyes for was Elizabeth.

Jacob was due to be at Frank's shop early the following morning, so he walked Elizabeth home after dinner, brought her up to her apartment, and let her father know how much he appreciated the hospitality he and his family had shown him. It was difficult to leave Elizabeth, but the knowledge that he would be back in less than a week's time made it less painful.

The following morning, Jacob showed up for work and was faced with a beaming Frank.

"Jacob, working with you the other day provided me with so many good surprises. I can't wait to see what you show me today."

Jacob did not disappoint. By the end of the day, as Jacob was leaving, Frank handed him more money than he had originally promised.

"Frank, I think you have made a mistake. There is too much money in my hand."

"Jacob, you are worth this and ten times more. You produce more work in a day than three men put together. On top of that, you are pleasant, honest, and kind. You may think it your blessing that brought you into my shop that day, but I feel the blessing is mine. Drive home safely. I'll see you in a few days."

Once again, Jacob stopped at Shlomo's to pick up his car and headed for Boston. This time, he decided he would not make a side trip to the diner to see Louis and Rachel. There would be lots of opportunities to see them again, but this time, he just wanted to get home as quickly as possible to call Elizabeth and say goodnight. Yes, this was a man in love.

Chapter 30

A Real Family

Summer was ending, and Labor Day fast approaching. The shop in Boston would be closed for the long holiday weekend, so Heschel was invited to New York for the family Sabbath dinner on Friday evening and to tour the city with Jacob and Elizabeth. It would be the first time Heschel was meeting Elizabeth, but the happiness that Jacob exuded was contagious.

Many people from the city spent the summers at the shore and would be moving back on Labor Day weekend. Frank told Jacob he could have that particular week off so that he could spend the time with his brother and Elizabeth's family. Frank had, at that point, also become like family. Jacob couldn't wait to introduce Heschel to him.

Jacob and Heschel arrived at Shlomo's on Friday afternoon. Heschel had heard so much about Shlomo and vice versa. The three men sat around and told stories about each other, drank schnapps, and munched on crackers and chopped liver. The afternoon went by, and it was time to pick up Elizabeth and her father.

Jacob could hardly contain his excitement at introducing Heschel to Elizabeth. This was a family unlike any that Heschel had ever been part of. Certainly, it was not like Max and Esther.

Mr. Levy opened the door with a warm welcome and a hearty handshake. "Hello, Heschel, and welcome to my home."

The electricity was in the air, and Heschel could finally see what Jacob had been so excited about all these weeks. As soon as Elizabeth came into the room and gave Heschel the warmest hug and kiss on the cheek, he was convinced. This is the way it is supposed to be. This is what a real family is supposed to act like. His happiness for Jacob was all-consuming.

They walked the blocks down the street to Aunt Evelyn's house, and Heschel experienced the same feelings that Jacob had at the first Shabbos dinner. Since the day his mother had died, Heschel had not experienced the joy of welcoming the Sabbath and the love that the family exuded reached out to him as well.

The rest of the weekend was equally as wonderful. Elizabeth brought Jacob and Heschel to Saturday-morning services at her temple and introduced them to practically the whole congregation. This had become so foreign to both boys. They really had no religious upbringing once their mother was gone. After the morning service, they joined the rest of the congregation in a beautiful luncheon in the great hall.

Everyone had their eyes on Jacob and Elizabeth. Jacob and Elizabeth only had their eyes on each other. Of course, every now and then, an observant mother would approach Heschel and tell him about her "very beautiful" and "single" daughter.

Unlike Jacob, Heschel was tall and handsome. He had no idea how handsome he was and seemed to be oblivious to all the single women who swooned over him. He was as kind and gentle as Jacob, but his youth provided him with a naivete that did not go unnoticed. Jacob shielded Heschel as much as he could from all negative aspects of life.

Heschel remained bothered by his separation from Max but at the same time relieved. Every now and then, he would let Jacob know how he felt.

"Jacob, how can we abandon our father? How can we just walk away and pretend that he doesn't exist?"

As calm as could be, Jacob would respond, "Heschel, it is not us who has abandoned anyone. We have been as true to our father as two sons could be. It is he who has abandoned us when he had no use for us, and now that we are old enough to help him out with his life, he is trying to make you feel that you have abandoned him. I will never forgive him for walking away from us, but more importantly,

I will never forgive him for keeping us away from our mother while she was dying.

"He is and always has been an evil man, and that will never change. You and I have now been exposed to how a loving family should be. If I am fortunate enough to make a life with Elizabeth, it will be a life fashioned after that. My children will always feel loved and protected. Heschel, the onus of responsibility was never on you. It was never on me. Our father owed us love and protection, and we got neither. Do not feel guilty. Feel relieved that you now have the life you deserve."

On Sunday, Jacob and Elizabeth took Heschel to Coney Island and made him go on the roller coaster along with them, and Heschel practically passed out as they disembarked.

"Oh my god, sailing the seas from Europe to America was bad enough, but this was terrifying. Please, Jacob, do not make me do this again."

Jacob was bent over from laughing so hard. Heschel had never before seen this side of his brother. He decided then and there that he would go on ten more roller coaster rides if it brought this much glee to Jacob—well, maybe.

By Monday afternoon, Jacob and Heschel left for Boston. Jacob decided to stop by and check on Louis and Rachel on the way home. He definitely had an ulterior motive for this as well. He really wanted Heschel to meet Rachel.

On the ride, Heschel extolled his feelings about Elizabeth and her family. "Jacob, I am so happy for you. Elizabeth is wonderful, and the love she has for you is so apparent. Her family is equally as inviting and so welcoming. Do not wait too long to bring us all together again."

This was more than Jacob could ever have wished for. Heschel even loved meeting Frank and enjoyed the collaboration the two men had. Yes, life was turning out fine for Jacob, and Heschel would soon follow. The promise of America was turning out as hoped.

Two very short hours later, the boys had talked nonstop, and Jacob pulled into a petro/diner station. When Jacob got out of the car, Louis came running out.

"Jacob, Jacob!" he yelled. "I have not seen you in a while. How are you?"

With that, Jacob and Heschel were ushered into the diner. Rachel was behind the counter, and her eyes lit up at the sight of Jacob.

"Jacob, it has been so long. You look well. I am so happy to see you."

Jacob introduced Rachel to Heschel, explaining that he was his brother whom he had brought to New York to meet his girlfriend's family. The sparkle somewhat left Rachel's eyes when she heard this, but nevertheless, she was as cordial and friendly to Jacob's brother as could be.

Yes, he was very handsome, but he was not Jacob. Her heart fell. In spite of this, she smiled and served. She kept on a lively conversation even though her heart was broken. Rachel, to no avail, was smitten.

After they left the diner, Heschel was very firm with Jacob. "Do you not see how this woman feels about you? It is not me she wants to fix up with. She is so smitten with you."

"Nonsense. She knows about Elizabeth and how I make these weekly treks to New York."

"Nevertheless," said Heschel, "she only has eyes for you."

There was no way that Jacob could ever consider anyone other than Elizabeth. She was the light of his life.

Chapter 31

Too Close for Comfort

Boston was a city that was changing by the day. Everything was catching up to technology and science. Even the women were different. Hair was cut shorter, dresses were shorter, and a lot was more relaxed. Yet it had a lot of time to go before it caught up to New York. New York seemed to be the nucleus of style and culture. In Jacob's world, Elizabeth was *his* nucleus of New York.

The fall went by, and Thanksgiving was fast approaching. Jacob was in New York every week, and he and Elizabeth had a secret understanding that they would announce their engagement on New Year's Eve. Jacob was so excited and so in love.

At Thanksgiving, Jacob and Heschel arrived with bread puddings and lemon curd pie, along with hearty appetites. Aunt Evelyn hosted this holiday, and the amount of food was staggering: two turkeys, dressing, potatoes, vegetables, and all kinds of breads. Yes, this was a gastronomic experience. Jacob was so excited at the impending engagement announcement. Yet it was still several weeks away.

As Jacob held Elizabeth's hand, he noticed a stillness in her eyes. "Elizabeth, my love, are you feeling all right?"

"Jacob, I'm just a little tired. The holidays have taken a lot out of me."

Jacob was, after all, an observer, and did not buy any of this. "Elizabeth, I am leaving right now and taking you to the hospital. You should not be sick, but we are going to get to the bottom of this."

Surprisingly, Elizabeth did not object. She allowed Jacob to wrap her in a blanket and take her to the hospital.

"I'm sure this is nothing serious, but I do not like the way you look," Jacob said. "I feel better taking this approach. Dinner will carry on without us."

Jacob explained to the family that Elizabeth was not feeling well and that it was in her best interest to get her to emergency. Not to worry, he assured them, just a precaution.

Her pallor was almost white, and Jacob had never been so frightened in his life.

My Elizabeth, I took so long to find you. Please be well. Please make me make you well.

After two hours, the doctor came out and told Jacob that Elizabeth's experience with tuberculosis had weakened her lungs, and even a slight cold could be dangerous. He did not feel that it was any worse than that at this point, but to be on the safe side, he would like her to stay overnight and get some oxygen and medicine into her. Her breathing was shallow, but he was certain she would recover.

"Doctor, please, whatever it takes, whatever you need, don't let her die."

Jacob was a desperate man in a very desperate situation. He could only think of the worst scenario. How could God have played such a terrible trick on these two people so in love? As convincing as the doctor tried to be, Jacob could only think the worst.

Elizabeth needed rest, so Jacob went back to Aunt Evelyn's house. Everyone there was on pins and needles, waiting for the report on Elizabeth. Jacob played it down as much as he could. She had had relapses before that were much worse. She would get through this one as well. Her father saw the fear in Jacob's eyes and was not convinced.

They got through dinner, and Heschel and Jacob walked Mr. Levy home with the promise to be back in the morning to accompany him to the hospital. When the boys got back to the rooming house, they filled Shlomo in on the night's events. Jacob was so happy to not be alone. Having his brother and good friend there was a blessing. They stayed up and talked until Jacob's eyes could no longer stay open.

"I must get to sleep so that the morning will come faster. Good night!" he shouted out as he climbed the stairs to his room.

Sleep still did not come easy for Jacob, and he was up and dressed shortly after dawn. It would still be awhile before he could visit Elizabeth, but he put a call in to the nurses' station. Elizabeth had an uncomfortable night and needed much oxygen, but her color was coming back and she was resting easy.

Jacob breathed a sigh of relief and ran to the kitchen to make himself a cup of coffee. He still had several hours to go before he could pick up Mr. Levy and see Elizabeth for himself. He decided to leave and take a long walk in the brisk fall air.

As he passed the diner where he originally had his first date with Elizabeth, he broke down in tears.

"Please!" he shouted to the heavens. "Do not take her from me."

He continued down the street as people were coming out of their houses. He felt less alone watching the day's activities begin for so many people. They all looked happy. It was the day after Thanksgiving, which was considered a school holiday. Children came pouring out of their houses, and life was abound. No one could ever have guessed the sadness in the heart of this man walking down the street.

By ten o'clock in the morning, Jacob went back to the rooming house and picked up Heschel. Together they got Mr. Levy and headed for the hospital. By the time they approached Elizabeth's room, they saw a rosy-cheeked girl with a big grin on her face. Between the rest, the care, and the oxygen, she was recovering. She would have to take it easy for a few days, but she was on the mend.

"Oh my god, Elizabeth, you gave us such a fright." Jacob took her in his arms and held her as tight as he could.

Happiness was back, and then and there, he made a quick decision.

"Elizabeth," he whispered in her ear. "I don't want to wait till New Year's Eve to announce our engagement. Can't we tell them sooner, like right away? I want to get you a beautiful ring and announce to the world that we're in love and want to get married. We waited so long to be together, and life is so short. I don't want to waste another minute of my life without you."

Beaming, Elizabeth nodded and held Jacob's hand as hard as she could.

"Now let's get you home to your own surroundings."

Mr. Levy was so overcome with relief. He had been down this road before, and it never got any easier.

"I think Aunt Evelyn owes me a turkey dinner. I am starving."

As soon as Jacob got Elizabeth home and made her comfortable, he called the family to let them know the events of the day. Aunt Evelyn was thrilled to pack up a huge care package for her niece. Heschel picked it up for them and found that the inquisition was waiting for him. He thought he would just pick up the food and get right back; however, that was not the case.

"So tell me," Aunt Evelyn said through her wide grin, "how come a young, handsome boy like yourself is not yet taken? We have so many attractive Jewish women here that would love to be fixed up with you. You wouldn't even need a matchmaker. You could be like a kid in a candy store. Just leave it up to me."

It was not unusual in those days for families to hire a matchmaker to find a mate for their children. Families often agreed on these things as soon as the children were born. A lot had to do with their social standing in the community and, for the women, the size of their dowry.

Heschel, not wanting to feel ungrateful, lied, probably for the first time in his life, and told Aunt Evelyn that as much as he appreciated her thoughts and efforts, he already had someone in mind back in Boston. Her disappointment was palpable.

"Aunt Evelyn," he said. "I know that Elizabeth is wanting to make up for missing your wonderful Thanksgiving feast, and I really should get this food back so she can begin building up her strength. If things do not work out back at home, you will be the first one I call. Let this be our little secret."

With this, she wrapped her arms around Heschel and gave him the biggest hug. He thought she would never let go. No one had ever shared such a secret with her before, and she felt honored. Yes, this would be their little conspiracy. She found that she liked him as much as she liked Jacob. They were two fine boys.

Heschel sprinted back to Elizabeth's house with a huge container of Thanksgiving goodies. Elizabeth was sitting up in the living room and seemed to be on the mend. Her eyes lit up when she surveyed the food Heschel had brought back. Although she ate like a bird, every bite was an encouragement to Jacob. This turned out to be nothing more than a mild cold, but with her delicate condition, this could someday turn deadly.

Heschel regaled them all with the tale of Aunt Evelyn, aka the matchmaker. Once Elizabeth had finished what she wanted, she and Jacob called Mr. Levy and Heschel into the room and announced their engagement. After Mr. Levy stopped crying, he hugged his daughter and explained that his tears were tears of joy, but also, he wished her mother had been there to share this happy time.

Heschel was also so overjoyed. Much planning would have to be made before a wedding could take place. Where would they make their home? What would happen to the shop in Boston? What about Frank? What about Elizabeth leaving her family to move, unless, of course, Jacob made the decision to move to New York? Boston was the only home Jacob knew of, yet New York was the only home to Elizabeth as well. Her father would be alone.

There were so many things to consider, but for the time being, a glass of wine needed to be raised and the celebration needed to take place.

By Sunday morning, Elizabeth seemed to be back to her old self. Jacob decided to go back to Boston with Heschel early instead of beginning the week with Frank. It seemed as though ages had passed since he had been back to his shop.

He called Frank, who was very understanding, and promised he would get back on the old schedule by the end of the week. He left Elizabeth to make all the phone calls that were necessary to announce her engagement to her family. Jacob was ten feet off the ground as he kissed her goodbye and left for home.

Chapter 32

Back to Reality

The ride back to Boston seemed to go so easy with Heschel at Jacob's side.

"Jacob, I could not be happier than I am right now. You have found a real family to belong to, and Elizabeth is a wonderful woman. I hate to bring this up, but after all, Max is still your father. I know we both have been estranged from him and Esther for several months now, but perhaps this time he has softened a bit. After all, he now has a young child and a wife by his side. I will go along with whatever decision you make, but think long and hard before you cut him out from your wedding."

"Heschel, our father did not soften when he abandoned us for years in Eastern Europe. He never welcomed us with open arms when we came to this country. Total strangers welcomed us ten times more than our own flesh and blood did. I will never forget what he called Elizabeth when I first went to New York. He didn't even know her, yet he presumed she was a hussy. He makes everything black and dismal."

"No, Heschel, I will never blame you for having him in your life, if you so choose, but I will never allow him to tarnish the relationships I have formed with Elizabeth's loving family. He is out of my life forever. I think of him and Esther as a disease that needs to be cut out. I will never change my mind."

It had been a very long time since Heschel had seen this side of Jacob. He knew that Jacob was a very kind person with a very forgiving nature, but there was no bending his feelings on this subject. Although he did not know about the "incident" at Jordanna's, there were two people who would never get forgiveness from Jacob, and his own father was one of them. As far as Esther went, she was nothing to him anyway, but he had a half-brother in the picture whom he may get to know years down the road, but for now, he wanted nothing to do with that whole family. Subject closed.

Monday morning, Jacob and Heschel went back to work. Jacob was impressed at the condition of the shop since he had been spending so much time in New York. Heschel had hired a wonderful young man who just wanted to learn the trade, and surprisingly, he picked it up very quickly. Anthony Cardone's family had emigrated from Italy. They had settled in the north end of Boston when Anthony was very young, so he spoke English very well. He was eighteen years old, had graduated high school, and was a hard and diligent worker. He loved working for Heschel and Jacob and inhaled all the knowledge they shared with him. He was becoming quite a tradesman.

What also did not go unnoticed was his value system. He was very family oriented and was devoted to his parents, brothers, and sisters. The three men got along great, and all the customers who came into the shop loved dealing with them. As well as the Jewish trade, Anthony spread the word through his Italian neighborhood. Business was booming.

By Friday, Jacob was back at Frank's shop. He could hardly contain himself when he bolted through the door, slapped Frank on the back, and told him how his holiday had turned out. Frank was so happy for him but was now concerned about losing Jacob to Boston. Jacob insisted that even if he and Elizabeth settled in Boston, they would be back every month to see family and Jacob would always make himself available to Frank whenever he needed him. It seemed to Frank that everything was happening so fast, but he could never know the years lost between Jacob and Elizabeth. They had so much time to make up for. Jacob had never been surer of anything in his life.

The next few weeks sped by. Jacob went back to his old job of working with Frank. This was becoming second nature to him. He loved seeing Elizabeth every week and making sure she stayed strong. The fright that he had over Thanksgiving was something he did not want to relive.

"Jacob," said Mr. Levy, "every now and then, Elizabeth will come down with a cold, and it may turn into pneumonia. Tuberculosis did quite a number on her lungs and weakened them. It will be up to you to look over her and keep her healthy."

"Mr. Levy, there is nothing in the world I would not do to protect her. You can feel safe when she is with me."

Before they knew it, New Year's Eve was approaching. Jacob could never have imagined last year that he would be spending this New Year's with Elizabeth by his side. Jacob was in New York, and Frank and his wife had invited Elizabeth and him to join them in a huge feast at their home.

It was a wonderful evening. Frank's whole family was there, and at midnight, they all counted down the clock. Jacob took Elizabeth in his arms and had never felt so much joy and hope for the future. Wedding plans were in the works. They had decided on an April wedding, would honeymoon in the Catskills, and live in Boston.

"Pinch me, sweetheart," he whispered in Elizabeth's ear. "How did I get so lucky?"

"No," she protested. "*I* am the lucky one."

This was probably the biggest dispute they had.

Chapter 33

Love Is in the Air

Jacob had never felt such contentment in his life. Business was going great, he had the love of his life, and he had found a new family to love. He brought Heschel into the fold as much as possible, but Heschel had his own demons to address. He could not totally dismiss Max and Esther. Jacob had never disclosed to him the horror he experienced while at Jordanna's. The shame, although it was not his fault, never left his mind. All Jacob wanted to do was protect Heschel. He loved him more than a brother; he loved him as though he were his child.

Business in Boston was going great—so great, in fact, that Jacob took some liberties and would leave for New York each week a little earlier than usual.

Heschel understood this and never complained. After all, his brother was engaged to be married, and he really liked—no, loved—the extended family. Heschel only hoped that he would soon meet someone to bring him the amount of happiness that was allotted Jacob.

Jacob was still staying at Shlomo's rooming house. At the same time, he was scouring apartments in Boston. He loved bringing a bottle of schnapps one day a week and tying one on with Shlomo. They would talk and laugh until they could no longer keep their eyes open. Amazing what life brings to us. These two had become as close as brothers.

Life had suddenly presented a certain rhythm to Jacob's life. Marriage plans were in the works, bridal showers were being planned, but most importantly, after April, he and Elizabeth would never be separated again.

Jacob finally found the perfect apartment. It was on the top floor of a two-family home facing the ocean in South Boston. South Boston had become known as the Irish part of the city, but Jacob, the optimist, felt that he could get along with anyone. Boston, after all, was becoming a melting pot of people.

Jacob absolutely felt that he could belong anywhere. The bottom line was the fact that Elizabeth would always have the ocean at her feet. It was important to Elizabeth to be near the water. For whatever reason, she found the ocean calming and had always loved to have it near. The fact that she would now be able sit out on her own front porch and overlook the beach gave her an exhilarated feeling. Everything was falling into place, and she would soon be Mrs. Jacob Kalinsky. She could not have hoped for more.

As for Jacob, his past was his past, and he tried valiantly to put it behind him. He would never fully escape the scars from his years in Europe or his beginnings in America, but to be able to go from the depths of despair to being on top of the world in a single lifetime was almost beyond belief.

The festivities prevailed. All of Elizabeth's cousins made prebridal parties for her. Jacob, Heschel, Shlomo, and Frank were always part of these celebrations along with their wives or partners. Everyone loved Jacob and respected him and wanted only goodness in his life going forward. This was a part of Jacob's future that he could never have imagined. Elizabeth was his whole world, and nothing or no one would take this away from him.

It was an understood practice during this time in life that young women would live with their fathers until they married. It was understood that Elizabeth would move from her father's home to her husband's. So it was that Jacob was still staying at Shlomo's and Elizabeth at home with her father when the call came in.

Trying to understand the mindset of someone who had experienced such horror to now experience such joy might have been an enigma to many, but Jacob was so consumed with his love for Elizabeth that nothing else mattered. It is so difficult to report how blindsided Jacob was when Elizabeth suddenly became ill. It was shortly after the Ides of March, a little more than one month prior to their wedding, that Elizabeth called for Jacob to be at her side.

"Don't be silly!" he exclaimed. "You have had a slight setback but will be fine in the morning."

Jacob boiled large pots of water so that Elizabeth could inhale the steam. He called the doctor, who instructed him to pound on her back to loosen up any inflammation. Both these things seemed to help.

"I am here by your side and will never leave you."

"Jacob, what if I die without ever experiencing making love to you?"

Being 1927, premarital sex was greatly frowned upon, and Jacob and Elizabeth had made a pact to save that special time for their wedding night.

Jacob cradled Elizabeth as close to his body as he could. "My darling, I have made love to you over and over in my mind. I could not be any closer to you than I am right now. Our wedding night will not diminish what I feel for you right now."

During the night, Elizabeth's breathing became more labored. Jacob would cry out, "Please breathe," but Elizabeth could not hear. By morning, Elizabeth had taken her last breath.

The guttural sound coming from Jacob's gut could not be construed as anything other than what it was. It was the sound of loss, of death, but it could never convey the amount of grief that Jacob was feeling. How unfortunate that it took so long for these two to reconnect. How most unfortunate that they came to realize that they knew they loved each other years before that. It was a monumental loss of time that they could never make up.

Jacob's cries were so loud that Mr. Levy woke up out of a sound sleep and came running into Elizabeth's room. Realizing what had happened, he dropped to his knees with cries almost as loud as Jacob's.

The ambulance arrived shortly, but to no avail. Elizabeth was gone. Jacob was wrapped so tightly around her body that the ambulance drivers could not peel her away.

"Breathe, breathe!" he shouted over and over. "I forbid you to leave me."

All he could do was rock back and forth with Elizabeth in his arms.

Finally, the drivers were able to take her away. Jacob was beyond consoling. Mr. Levy was not much better. This neighborhood was like a small village, and word passed within minutes throughout that something disastrous had taken place at the Levy home. Before long, the entire family was there. Everyone was in disbelief.

It is customary to have a speedy burial in the Jewish faith, often within the first twenty-four hours of death. It is believed that once the soul leaves the body, it hovers around in a state of limbo until it is laid to rest. When the body returns to the dust, from where it is believed to have come, the soul is then free to return to heaven.

It is believed that this is for the good of the departed; however, it is also believed that it is best for the people mourning.

Chapter 34

Back to Hell

The following day, the mourners poured into the synagogue to attend the service for Elizabeth. Heschel came to Jacob as soon as he heard, but no one could absorb any of his pain. The chapel was filled to capacity with people pouring out into the street. The Levys were a much-loved family, and Elizabeth was so highly regarded for all her sweetness and kindness that shopkeepers closed their stores for the day to support Elizabeth's family, most of all Jacob. He was inconsolable.

The ride behind the hearse seemed endless. Finally, they arrived at the cemetery, and it seemed that the entire congregation had followed. Elizabeth's coffin was put into place, but not before Jacob threw himself over it, crying like a wounded animal.

"Take me with you!" he screamed.

No one faulted him; in fact, there was not a dry eye to be had.

After the mourner's kaddish was recited, shovels were picked up, and dirt was placed over her coffin. This may seem like a brutal thing to do, but the pain of hearing the dirt hit the coffin brings the pain of bereavement to the surface. This is the most painful part of the process, but a necessary one. It is the beginning of the grieving process, and this is the only way that healing can begin.

No one left until the last shovel was laid to rest. People poured out of the cemetery, but Jacob could not allow himself to leave. It was sundown before he left the love of his life buried beneath the dirt and flowers. He was a lost soul.

Then follows seven days of shiva. The family cover all mirrors in the home, sit on boxes, wear no shoes, and do not shave or apply makeup while neighbors, friends, and extended family come to show their respect. Since Jacob was not yet Elizabeth's husband, he was not considered an actual mourner, but no one could dismiss the fact that his grief was the greatest. He sat with the family the entire time, and at night, he would sleep in Elizabeth's bed.

How, he asked himself, *can I leave here and leave her?*

Her scent prevailed in her bed, and Jacob would bury his face in her pillow and dream that she was really there. In the morning, the realization of what was real hit, and once again, the unbearable pain set in.

Jacob's only consolation was sleeping in Elizabeth's bed, getting her scent on whatever he was wearing so he could preserve it. After three weeks, Mr. Levy and the rest of the family sat him down.

"Jacob, you have a career to attend to and family back in Boston. You cannot dwell on what was, and you must put it in its proper place and begin to move on. We all love you and want you to know that you will always have a home to come to here, but you have to move on with your life. Heschel needs you back to work and home. We all think it is time for you to move on."

All this being said was a shock to Jacob's system. He was nowhere near ready to move on. Perhaps Elizabeth's family could also not move on until he left.

"I know what I must do, but it is so hard for me to comprehend going back to Boston without my bride. I waited so long to find her, and now there is nothing. Please let me come and visit whenever I want. You have become my real family now, and I don't want to lose you."

"Jacob, we have come to think of you as one of our own. You will always be welcome here, but you must move on with your life."

The following day, Jacob packed up his belongings, along with Elizabeth's pillow, and headed for home. The ride was a blur. One month ago, he was on top of the world, and now he was living in such a dark void.

Why, he asked God, *am I so cursed? Other than Heschel, I have no real family of my own. Elizabeth was my family, and now I am once again alone.*

These thoughts were running through Jacob's mind as he was driving home and pulled off the road at the diner that was so familiar to him.

Chapter 35

A Familiar Place

As Jacob pulled up to the petro pumps, Louis came running out. He recognized Jacob's car and approached him with a warm embrace. As soon as he saw Jacob's face, he knew something was terribly wrong.

"Jacob, please come in, sit down, and let me make you something to eat. You look terrible."

Jacob was limp as Louis brought him into the diner.

"Jacob, what has happened?"

Jacob proceeded to pour his heart out as Louis listened intently. Through the heavy sobbing, Jacob told Louis everything that had gone on in the last seven years regarding his arriving in this country, meeting Elizabeth, reconnecting, and everything after that.

Louis listened with the heavy heart of a father. He let Jacob spill it all out, everything about his own miserable family from start to finish. Jacob let it all out except for that one incident at Jordanna's. That he would take to his grave. He never got over the shame he felt at that episode.

After a couple of hours and a few strong drinks, Louis was able to convince Jacob to spend the night. He made sure that Jacob first called Heschel to let him know that he would not be home that evening but he was, nevertheless, in good hands.

The following morning, Jacob awoke with a start. He found himself in unfamiliar surroundings.

What happened last night that I am now here?

Then it all came running back to him. Elizabeth was gone, he was on his way home, and for whatever reason, he was now with Louis.

Jacob went downstairs and entered the diner. Rachel was behind the counter and was not surprised to see Jacob. Her father had filled her in on everything.

"Jacob, I am so sorry to hear of your loss. If there is anything at all that either me or my father can do for you, please let us know. I cannot imagine the grief you are feeling."

"Rachel, thank you. I sort of tumbled in last night without a head on my shoulders, but your father was wonderful. I think I needed to be separate from the situation to see clearly. I am a man in mourning, but knowing that I have great friends and a wonderful support will help. Actually, I think I'm hungry. I am ready for a couple of eggs and toast."

With that, Rachel busied herself to make Jacob the best breakfast he could ever have imagined. Jacob picked at his food, although the hot coffee was comforting. It was an amazing realization that he had this oasis to rest his head on before heading home. Life is mysterious. Without wandering into their diner several months ago, he never would have formed this friendship. Sad as he was, he knew he was fortunate enough to have this amazing support system, even though it was in the middle of a long, dark road leading home.

Jacob ended up spending the rest of the day at the diner, helping Louis out with the pumps and attending to the kitchen. He found this cathartic, and it took his mind off Elizabeth even if for a few moments.

It turned out that Louis had his own tale of woe to tell. Before Rachel was born, his wife had given him another baby. It was also a little girl, and after two boys, he was elated. It was a difficult birth, and his wife barely made it through. She developed a blood clot in her lung, and things were touch and go for many weeks.

His wife was the love of his life, and Louis could not bear the thought of raising this new child without a mother. While his wife was in the hospital, Louis awoke one morning, and as he checked on the baby, he saw she was blue. She had just died in her sleep.

The doctors told Louis that this was not unusual in the first several months of a child's life. It was just an unexplained death. In the meantime, his wife was still unimaginably ill, and he had to mourn alone. He couldn't even bring himself to tell her that they had lost their newborn baby. How could he face living life without his precious wife?

"Please, God!" he yelled to the sky. "How much suffering can one man endure? Please make her well."

It took some time, but little by little, Janice—Louis's wife—began to show improvement. Eventually, she was able to leave the hospital and return home, but her sickness and the loss of her baby had taken its toll on both of them. Sometimes, near death is almost as difficult to get over as the actual thing. If it happened once, it can happen again without warning.

Jacob was able to empathize with him over this. Louis still had his family, albeit he lost a child. Two years after losing their baby daughter, Janice realized she was pregnant again. Jacob would give anything to have had at least one year together with Elizabeth.

Louis tried to convince Jacob that it would only have been more difficult. Jacob was still young and ultimately would meet someone else and have a future. He assured him that he would never stop loving the memory of Elizabeth but that he eventually would find a place in his heart for another.

This was a whole new side of Louis that Jacob had not been aware of. It was then that the kinship formed between the two men.

"Louis, would it be all right if I stayed just one more night? The thought of going back home right now is devastating to me. I had imagined it would be to my new home with Elizabeth, and now I need to get strong enough to face my future without her. It is calming for me to be here and talk to you."

"Of course, Jacob. Stay as long as you like."

Chapter 36

Going Home

Two weeks had passed before Jacob finally felt strong enough to face Boston. He couldn't have been more grateful to Louis, Rachel, and Janice for their support and hospitality. He had many hours to sit and get to know Janice. She was a strong woman, and he always felt a little better after his talks with her.

She lived in the house behind the diner and for the most part spent most of her time there. The baby had been buried in their backyard, and a small monument was placed by her grave. There was not a day that she did not go out and speak to the baby she never got to know.

Jacob also spent some time pumping gas, working around the kitchen helping Rachel, and staying busy with what he considered simple work. Although he was still a broken man, there were some cracks coming through. Having this time with these three caring people made him feel less alone, and the dark cloud was starting to rise.

He stayed in touch with Mr. Levy and the rest of the family in New York so that they would not worry. They cared so deeply for him. This was the family he had always hoped for, and even without Elizabeth, he would never discount them as anything other than family to him.

Finally, he was on the way home to Heschel. Still, he could never fathom moving into the South Boston apartment without Elizabeth. He called the landlady and explained the situation, and she was very understanding. It was a great apartment with a water view and would rent again easily.

The ride back to Boston was not easy but a lot better than it would have been two weeks back. The stop at Louis's diner gave him some healing time. The pain, although excruciating at times, was a little lighter than it had been two weeks ago. Yes, it was time to get on with his life. Louis and his family could not have been kinder. Jacob left with the promise that he would not be a stranger and would return for a visit in the coming weeks.

As soon as Jacob got to the city, he stopped at the shop to see Heschel.

Poor Heschel, he thought. *I have left him high and dry. Now that I am back, I will make up for all the time I have been gone.*

What else was there for him to do now that Elizabeth was gone? Throwing himself into his work would be cathartic and take his mind off his loss.

"Jacob!" Heschel cried out as soon as he saw him come through the door. "I am so happy to see you. Anthony and I have done the best we could to keep things afloat, but it is your expertise that has been missing. What has happened is awful, but we are here for you now and will do whatever it takes to make it as easy for you as possible. Take as much time as you need."

With that, Heschel put his arms around his brother and kept him in a very-much-needed embrace.

Jacob filled Heschel in on the past two weeks and let him know how grateful he was to Louis's family for all their support. He had not yet had a moment alone, and for that he was grateful. Now it was time to go back to his old life and bury himself in his work. At least he was back with his brother, who had always been there for him.

"Jacob, I must confess that I have been in touch with Max and Esther. I have told them everything, and I truly think that they feel bad about what has happened. Would you consider going to see them now?"

"Heschel, erasing them from my life was like cutting out a cancer. Please do not think unkindly of me, but my father is dead to me, and if I want any semblance of peace going forward, it has to remain that way. I would never deny you having a relationship with them, but a person doesn't suddenly become someone he is not. I am happy for you to have them back in your life if that is what you want, but I never want to hear their names mentioned. I hope it's true, that they have softened, but please beware. A leopard does not change his spots."

Jacob felt sad that his brother would be left with the burden of their father, but it was now time for Jacob to think about what was in his best interest going forward in life. Certainly, being around Max and Esther was useless and a waste of time he could never regain. Many lessons were learned from losing Elizabeth, mainly that time was precious and he had to fill it with positive situations and positive people.

The next month was an absolute blur to Jacob. He went through the mechanics of going to work, eating his meals, and sleeping with dreams of Elizabeth. Every morning, he would awake with a start. Once he was fully awake, he would shake the dreams from his head, run into the shower, get dressed, have his coffee, and go back to work. This schedule became rote for him. Nothing changed.

After what seemed like forever, Jacob finally awoke with a slightly lighter heart. Elizabeth was the greatest chapter in his life, and if he were to ever have any semblance of happiness again, he would have to find the place in his heart that he could carry her memory around forever, but find another way to regain some happiness.

He immediately went to the phone and called Shlomo.

"Hi, my old friend. I was wondering if you might have my old room ready for a couple of days."

"Jacob! How wonderful to hear from you. You have been on my mind every day, and I was hoping you would call. How are you doing?"

"Well, my dear friend, I have not been doing so well, but it is time to pull it together and put my grief in its proper place. I would like to come to NY next weekend and visit with Mr. Levy and see the rest of Elizabeth's family."

"Jacob, you will always have a place to stay with me. I can't wait to see you."

"I will arrive on Friday afternoon and see if Aunt Evelyn would be willing to have me for Shabbos dinner. I will even see if Frank needs a worker for Sunday. Going back for the first time will not be easy, but I must do this at some point."

Jacob then called Mr. Levy, who was delighted to hear from him. He let Jacob know that life has been awful ever since losing Elizabeth, but he was attending shul every morning and every night and managed to find some solace there. Having Jacob for a visit, even a short one, would bring some life back to his aching heart.

"I'll let everyone know that you are coming, and we'll plan a special Shabbos dinner. Oh, Jacob, this is the first time I have had reason to smile. Thank you for being in touch."

It had been weeks since Jacob had reason to smile. Being with Elizabeth's family would not be the same as with her there, but for now, it was the closest he could feel to her.

The next week dragged on, but Jacob threw himself into his work. The temple community heard about his latest tragedy, and the briskets began pouring in. It seemed as though every mother of every young woman over the age of seventeen had their eyes on Jacob. It was well-known up until now that he had been engaged to be married to a young woman from New York City. Now every mother wanted the opportunity for her daughter to be the first one to show how compassionate she could be for Jacob. Being a good listener and showing sorrow would surely catch his attention.

Jacob was still a man with a grieving heart, and these attentions did not go unnoticed, however how unwanted they were.

Heschel just kept shaking his head and smiling. "What are we going to do with all this food?"

This was the impetus that finally made Jacob decide it was time to pay New York a visit.

Finally, Friday morning rolled around, and Jacob made his way to New York. He decided to visit Louis and Rachel on the way back home. Their kindness helped him get through the first few weeks after Elizabeth's death, and he would forever be grateful for their hospitality.

Chapter 37

Revisiting

It was now May. As Jacob drove down the highway, his thoughts ran to what might have been. Had Elizabeth not passed, they would have been married by now. They would have gone on their honeymoon and would have been moved into their apartment. There would never have been a reason for them to be apart.

These thoughts made Jacob sad, and try as he might, he could not shake this sadness from his heart. It was too soon. He knew by now that he could survive and time would heal the pain. He opened the window and let the warm spring air filter into the car. The smell of spring would never be the same again.

This would be the first trip to the city without Elizabeth being there. So far, he was all right. He pulled up to Shlomo's rooming house and as he went in was greeted by his old friend.

"What? No schnapps today?"

"Do you have so little belief in me that I would ever forget something like that?"

With that, Jacob reached into his satchel and pulled out two bottles of whiskey. "I need to be awake and alert at Aunt Evelyn's tonight. Maybe one quick schnapps, but then I must go on to see Mr. Levy. I brought you two bottles in case I do not get back for a while."

Jacob remembered when he first met Shlomo. He made him feel so comfortable and welcomed. Everyone whom he came in contact with loved Jacob. He was such a good soul who wouldn't hurt a fly.

The time was getting late, and it would soon be Shabbos. Being spring, the days were longer and sundown would be later. He had just enough time to settle in, shower, and make it over to pick up Mr. Levy. He couldn't wait to see the family.

On his way to Mr. Levy's apartment, Jacob was hit with a sudden realization. The last time he walked these steps, Elizabeth had died. He stopped dead in his tracks and crossed the street. He just could not walk the same steps again without breaking down. Shortly, he reached the Levy home and rang the buzzer.

"Jacob!" Mr. Levy shouted as he bounded down the stairs.

He grabbed Jacob in a warm embrace, then looked him in the eyes and broke down sobbing. The two of them sobbed until the only thing left to do was laugh. Two grown men, standing on a stoop, holding each other up, and sobbing uncontrollably. What would Elizabeth have thought?

Once they got that out of their systems, they were able to just look each other in the eyes and shake their heads. No words needed to be said. Mr. Levy ran back into the foyer, got his hat, and came back out to put his arm through Jacob's and walk that way to Aunt Evelyn's house.

The whole family was there, and the excitement of seeing Jacob was palpable. It seemed as though part of Elizabeth was still in the family. Dinner was great, the wine plentiful, and before long, Jacob had quite a buzz on. He hadn't felt this good in a long time. The stories went around the table about Elizabeth as an awkward little girl. The night turned into a testimonial of her, a celebration of her life. Coming here was the best decision Jacob had made.

The evening lingered on, and Jacob promised to attend morning services with the family at shul.

When the evening finally came to an end, Jacob embraced everyone and walked Mr. Levy home.

"Jacob, you did a real mitzvah by coming here. A small part of Elizabeth came back to us tonight. You made the last year of her life the happiest."

"Mr. Levy, it was her light that shined on me. She gave me a family that I otherwise would never have. I am forever grateful for that. My hope is that our relationship continues to blossom and that I will always be welcome here."

"We are here for you for as long as you want us. You have become a very important part of our family, and we have no desire to ever let you go."

That being said, Jacob gave Mr. Levy one more embrace and promised to meet him in the morning to attend services.

Jacob slept soundly that night and awoke feeling a little lighter than when he first arrived. A part of Elizabeth would always be with him, and he would hang on to that feeling forever. A small place in his heart was dedicated to her and the effect she had on his life. He was feeling stronger and a bit happier than just a few days ago. Facing the future did not seem as dismal today.

He quickly got up, bathed, dressed, and headed out the door to meet Mr. Levy. Spring was in the air, and the trees looked more alive and fresher than he had remembered. As he and Mr. Levy walked to services, they reminisced about last night and what a cathartic experience it was for everyone.

The services were beautiful, and the rabbi made sure to give a special tribute to Elizabeth. He saw Jacob walking in and wanted to make this morning a little more special for his sake.

After services, lunch was served, and Jacob found that he could hardly chew a bite given the amount of attention he was getting from the entire congregation. Yes, this was beginning to feel more like home than home, but Heschel and his shop were still in Boston. He assured everyone that he would not be a stranger and left to go back to spend some time with Shlomo.

That evening, Jacob and Shlomo had dinner together in the rooming house kitchen. Shlomo, it turned out, was quite a chef. He prepared a dish of chicken paprikash with a recipe from the old country. This was passed down from his grandmother. He had prepared a wonderful soup and stuffed potatoes.

"If I keep getting fed like this, I will need a whole new closet full of clothes."

"Jacob," said Shlomo, "you are the best company I have had in a long time. Yes, the rooms here are usually full, but everyone is transient, and I don't form bonds with these people. From the moment you walked in, I felt an instant kinship. I love having you here, even without your own schnapps."

They both laughed, polished off the rest of the bottle Jacob had brought, and went to bed.

The following morning, Jacob showed up bright and early at Frank's shop. To say Frank was thrilled would be an understatement. They spent a good part of the day working, talking, laughing, and just enjoying the day. Late in the afternoon, Jacob bid Frank goodbye and headed back to Boston.

The weekend was coming to an end, and Jacob had to get back to his life. He had decided, however, to stop in and visit Louis and Rachel when he went through Connecticut. Thinking back to all the people who had come into his life as a result of Elizabeth was staggering. She had, after all, left a legacy. The tight bonds that were formed with everyone Jacob came in contact with was a tribute to his interest in other people. He was not just an observer, he was a great listener. People automatically knew they could trust him, and they did.

Chapter 38

Back to Connecticut

Jacob had called Louis before leaving New York to let him know that he would be stopping by. Unknown to him, or at least his unawareness, Rachel put on her prettiest dress, did her hair, put on a little makeup, and wore her brightest smile. She never really knew if she would see Jacob again, but she had hoped.

As Jacob approached the diner, Louis came running out. He was thrilled to see Jacob looking so much better than the last time he had seen him.

"Jacob, I was so happy to hear from you. Rachel has made us a wonderful supper, so let's go in the diner, sit down, and talk."

More food. Jacob was still full from the last dinner he had yesterday.

Why, he wondered, *does everyone want to feed me?*

As Jacob entered the diner, he was greeted by a bit more familiar version of Rachel. She ran up to him and gave him a huge hug. Naive as he still was, Jacob did not think of this as anything other than sisterly warmth.

They sat, talked, ate, and laughed a little, and when it began to get late, Jacob got up with a huge thank-you and promise to return.

"Jacob," Rachel said, "I plan to come to Boston next month to do some shopping. Perhaps you could spend some time and show me around?"

"Of course, Rachel. I would be delighted to. I'm sure Heschel would also like to join us. Let me know when you are coming in, and I'll plan a day for you to see the city."

Having Heschel join them was not exactly what Rachel had in mind, but she would, at least, be happy to see Jacob again. Little did she know that what Jacob had in mind was for her to get to know Heschel better.

During the next few weeks, Jacob found himself spending ten to fourteen hours a day in the shop. He worked until he could barely keep his eyes open, went home, and dropped into bed. The next morning, he would awake and begin the process all over again. This kept him from thinking and hurting.

There would be times that the cloud seemed to lift a little, but then his memory would attack like a knife, and the wound would open without mercy. When, he would think, will this dark cloud lift? Invitations from families from the temple kept pouring in. He was, after all, an eligible young man now. He had no interest in any of this and would politely decline all invitations.

Everyone told him that time would be his best healer. He would wish to escape to hibernation and awake after four more seasons passed. Perhaps then the pain would be gone. This, of course, was not likely to happen. He would have to go through the seasons, deal with the pain and loss, and ultimately move on. Hopefully, someday he would emerge from this nightmare and begin living again. In the meantime, work was his only salvation.

Heschel was helpless. He tried everything he could think of to be a good support for Jacob, but all Jacob wanted was to be left alone. When Heschel, Jacob, and Anthony worked in the shop together, the mood was a little lighter, and Heschel would begin to think that Jacob was getting back to his old self again. The day would ultimately end, and Jacob would come home, eat a small meal, and fall into bed.

While this was going on, Heschel was creating a life for himself. He was attending social events at the temple and community center. His good looks and seeming shyness were very appealing to most of the single young women there. Yes, Heschel was beginning to be seen as a catch. Jacob was oblivious to all this. He was too wrapped up in his own grief to notice.

It was because he never noticed that when Rachel finally came to town, and Jacob planned a day to meet Heschel at the Bunker Hill Monument, he was shocked to see that Heschel had brought a date.

"Jacob, Rachel, I would like you to meet Ariel."

Jacob, stunned, stuttered a quick "Hello." Rachel, almost giddy, gave Ariel a huge hug and welcomed her as though she were the insider and Ariel had just come into the fold. This day could not be any better.

The four of them climbed the steps of the monument and looked over the landscape until they could see forever. At one point, Rachel, being very short, asked Jacob to hold her up to the window so she could get a better look. This kind of closeness gave Rachel butterflies, but all Jacob could think of was Elizabeth. This was not her, nor could it ever be again.

Perhaps it was time for Jacob to take a second look at Rachel. She certainly was not wanting for looks. She was petite, with long, dark hair and a very pretty face. They already were friends, and he loved her parents. The thought of going out and meeting other women was not very appealing to him. Perhaps he could find some comfort with Rachel to see how things worked out. He certainly was not looking for a romantic relationship right now, but if it became common knowledge that he had a lady friend whom he spent time with, perhaps the "vultures" would leave him be.

It was an easygoing friendship, and Jacob felt at ease around Rachel. She knew about his past, and he did not have to make any excuses. This may not be such a bad thing, after all. Didn't Heschel tell him that he was certain Rachel liked him? He was not thinking of this as being a replacement for Elizabeth; there was no such thing, but at least a diversion so that when he came back to earth, it might make the landing a little less painful.

The rest of the day held unexpected fun. At times, Jacob felt so guilty because he was enjoying himself so much. He had never been out with Heschel before with two young women, and the girls really seemed to like each other. It was comfortable; it was easy. It was the way life should be. Lots of silliness and laughing.

They walked through the north end of Boston, saw the Old North Church, bought produce from the pushcarts, and walked the Freedom Trail. They stopped at the Union Oyster House for fish and chips and drank beer. Jacob couldn't remember when he last felt this alive. There was a carousel down by the pier, and they rode it around and around until they couldn't stand up anymore.

By the end of the day, Heschel and Ariel bid good night to Jacob and Rachel, and Jacob walked Rachel back to the rooming house that she was staying at.

"Jacob, I just had the best day. Thank you so much for showing me around. Tell me about Ariel. Are she and Heschel serious about each other?"

"Rachel, I was as shocked as you were to meet her. Heschel has never said one word about her to me. I will ask all my questions as soon as I get home. How about coming to my shop tomorrow? You can see where I spend all my time, and we can go to lunch before you catch your train to go back."

As happy as Rachel was at this thought, she also knew that Jacob needed time and space. "Thank you, Jacob. That would be very nice, but I have to get some things done tomorrow in the city and then must catch the train back to Connecticut. Perhaps next time."

Rachel may not have been a savvy young woman when it came to affairs of the heart, but it was her innate sense of what was proper and what was not that came forward in making this decision.

"All right then. Let me know when you arrive home. Good night."

With that, Jacob gave Rachel a brotherly hug and watched her go into the building.

Although Jacob felt a bit uneasy—and why, he did not know—he was sorry to see Rachel leave. They had a great day, and his mind had wandered from Elizabeth for the first time since she passed away. He was certainly not looking to fall into another relationship so soon, but it was comforting to have Rachel as a friend.

The next day, Jacob was back at work, but surprisingly, his mind would flee to Rachel. Why, he thought, did this make him feel guilty? Elizabeth was the love of his life, and he would never let her memory leave him, but she was no longer there. He had thought of Rachel as a good friend; however, they had such a good time over the weekend, and he wanted to do it again.

By nightfall, he picked up the phone to call Rachel to make certain she had arrived home. Louis answered the phone and let Jacob know that a very exhausted Rachel had stumbled into the house, hugged her father, and left to go to sleep.

What he could not possibly have known was that Rachel just wanted to be alone with her thoughts of the past two days. She knew that she had succeeded in throwing a thought Jacob's way and that possibly a flame had begun to flicker. If she played her cards right, then Jacob would not know what had hit him when it did. For now, she would be the compassionate friend whose shoulder he could lean on.

Patience, Rachel, patience, she would tell herself.

Chapter 39

Moving Forward

Jacob could not believe what a good time he had with Rachel, Heschel, and Ariel. For a brief moment, Elizabeth went to the recesses of his mind, and for that, he felt overwhelming guilt. It had only been a few months since she passed, and in his mind, he had no right to experience anything but sadness at this point. Still, he did allow himself to let go, and for that brief time, it felt good. Perhaps, in time, he would allow himself to feel again. For the time being, he could not wait to get home and hear what Heschel had to say for himself.

As soon as Jacob entered their apartment, Heschel grabbed his arm, sat him down, and spoke. "I know what you're going to say. Yes, Ariel and I have been seeing each other for several weeks now, and she is wonderful. I have not told you because I wanted you to have your grieving further in the past. I didn't question whether or not you would be happy for me. I just didn't want to make you any sadder than you already were.

"I also was aware that you wanted me to find a way to get to know Rachel better, but it is very clear that it is you she is interested in. If I told you that I was bringing Ariel today, then you might not have had Rachel come in, and I think that would have been a mistake. I hadn't seen you smile in months, and it felt so good to see us all together today actually enjoying ourselves."

"Heschel, in many respects, you are a lot smarter than your older brother. I am happy for you. Ariel seems like a very sweet girl, and she and Rachel really enjoyed each other's company. I am grateful for today, and I hope there will be more days like it to come. It will be a long time for me to be able to put Elizabeth in the past, but because of her, I now know what a loving relationship should be, and I do want to find that again. Thank you for always being there for me."

With that, the two brothers embraced and went to bed so they could begin fresh the next morning.

The following morning, Jacob arose for the first time without a heavy cloud hanging over his head. The past weekend had been cathartic in more ways than he could ever have imagined. He decided that he would follow up with a phone call to Rachel in the evening and perhaps make plans to see each other again. He did want to make another trip to New York to visit Elizabeth's family, so he would coordinate that with a trip to see Rachel on the way back.

Jacob stopped and picked up hot bagels and coffee on the way to the shop. Heschel was delighted to see the energy that he found over the weekend carried over to the week. Heschel loved Elizabeth and her family and was saddened at her death, but life is for the living, and he was happy to see life once again injected into his brother's being. Hadn't they both been through enough during their lifetime? At any rate, Heschel was falling for Ariel and was ecstatic that the four of them were able to have such a great time over the past weekend. His hope was that the feelings were mutual and that they would continue to grow.

Jacob let Heschel know that he would probably cut the week short and go to New York to have Shabbos dinner with Elizabeth's family on Friday night, and stop to see Rachel and her parents on the way back. Now that Anthony had become an integral part of the business, Jacob had more time to himself than ever before. His plan was to call Mr. Levy that evening and run his plans by him. Aunt Evelyn always welcomed him with open arms, anyway. Aside from Elizabeth, her family had become very close to him and replaced the family he never had from Max.

Many times, Heschel would bring up Max and Esther, but it was no use. On this subject, Jacob was adamant. They were dead to him. If Heschel and Ariel became a serious couple and he wanted to bring her to meet them, Jacob would never stand in his way, but Jacob still saw them as a poison that could ruin anything.

First thing next morning, Jacob called Mr. Levy and told him about his intended plan to come to New York.

"Oh, Jacob, I would love to see you next weekend, but I have been invited to my friend's home for the weekend on the island. Perhaps next week?"

Jacob was disappointed but was still happy for Mr. Levy that he was getting out and seeing people. "Yes, let's plan for dinner next week. Please let Aunt Evelyn know that I will be coming in. I miss your whole family and have come to consider them mine as well. I'll look forward to seeing you the following week."

After Jacob got off the phone, he thought about calling Rachel.

If I call Rachel and make a special trip to see her, it may give the wrong impression, he thought. *After all, I am still mourning the loss of Elizabeth.*

That being said, it occurred to him that he felt a kinship with Rachel that he did not expect. He would still call Rachel and make plans to stop by to see her and her father the following week on his way back from New York. Still, Jacob was storing a small place in his heart for someone other than Elizabeth, and this made him feel guilty. After all, they had never married, had never consummated their relationship, and how much time was required for him to mourn?

Jacob was trying to convince himself that it was all right to be attracted to someone else, even though it was pretty sudden. Of course, it wasn't the heart-thumping emotion that Jacob felt whenever he saw Elizabeth. It was a more comfortable, easy feeling. Definitely he was attracted to her. Rachel was a svelte beauty. Elizabeth was so much worldlier than her, but what should that matter? Jacob could not begin to compare one against the other. There would never be another Elizabeth in his life, but perhaps there could be room for Rachel.

At any rate, he knew he did not want to be alone. It was obvious by now that Rachel was attracted to him, and the thought of meeting women and courting them was so distasteful. Rachel was a jewel in the rough, and he would take the time to see where this would go.

First, he had to make plans to see her again. Didn't he, after all, have a wonderful time when she visited Boston? He actually hated to see her go.

Stop analyzing this. My mind can be so cynical at times. All this is, is a date. I will call Rachel up to see how she and her father are doing and make plans to meet them both for dinner. What harm could there possibly be in that?

After fighting with himself for over an hour, Jacob finally called Rachel. He was surprised at how happy he was to hear her voice.

"Hi, Rachel. It's Jacob. I just wanted to check in on you and your father and know that all is well. Reflecting on our weekend together, I thought about the surprise with Ariel and Heschel and thought you might like to be brought up to date."

After Jacob relayed what he knew, he then asked if he could come to Connecticut the following Saturday evening to take her to dinner.

Rachel's heart was soaring, but she could not let it come through. She was aware of what a delicate situation this was and how easy it would be for him to be on the rebound. She wanted Jacob to want to be with her and not just a replacement for Elizabeth.

"Jacob, how nice to hear from you. I'm sure that my father and I will both be here next Saturday evening and we would love to see you."

For some reason, this did not resonate the way Jacob had thought it would. In his mind, he had expected a jubilant Rachel to quickly respond with a resounding yes. However, her composure was evident, and this made Jacob even more eager to see her. Although he had included Louis in his initial invitation, he was half-hoping that it would be just he and Rachel.

Oh well.

Jacob was far from getting over Elizabeth but was smart enough to recognize how healing this diversion was.

The following week, Jacob drove to New York, picked up Mr. Levy, and spent Shabbos dinner with the rest of the family. Most of the conversation was still centered around Elizabeth, but the tone was a little more lighthearted than before.

The following morning, Jacob spent Shabbos services at the same temple he had been to so many times before with Elizabeth. A light lunch was served, and while there, he could not help but notice the fingers being pointed his way and the giggles of the young women. In mourning or not, he was still regarded as a catch, and all sense of proper conduct was gone. In his mind, he compared this to a horse race: the horses being lined up in their stalls, the gun going off, and the first one out of the stall was the winner.

Inside, he was laughing at the image of this, but no matter how unkind this thinking was, he was happy to be able to have this private joke among him and himself. In most Jewish communities, parents of young Jewish girls were always in a hurry to pair off their daughters as young as possible. This eliminated the fear of one's child becoming an "old maid." Things like this would never have occurred to Jacob before he met Elizabeth. She, her aunts, and her cousins filled him in on the mores of Jewish life in the Lower East Side.

After lunch, Jacob said his goodbyes to everyone and headed to Shlomo's for one last visit before he left to see Rachel. As always, Shlomo loved his visits from Jacob. He was not surprised that Rachel had come up on Jacob's radar but encouraged him to take it slow. After all, Elizabeth had not been gone that long, and he was guarding Jacob's heart as well as this young girl in Connecticut. It would be so easy to run into a new relationship on the rebound. This would not be good in any case. Jacob embraced Shlomo and promised to see him in a month's time.

The ride to Connecticut was so different this time. The heaviness was gone, and a new kind of excitement filled the air. Elizabeth would always be the love of his life, he kept reminding himself, but there had to be room for someone else. Rachel could very well be that person, but he had to take it slow. This is the thought that reverberated in his mind since seeing Shlomo.

At precisely 5:00 p.m., Jacob pulled into the diner's parking lot. As usual, Louis came running out to greet him.

"Jacob, it's been awhile. I am so happy to see you again. Come inside and let me make you a hot cup of tea."

As soon as Jacob entered the diner, a radiant Rachel came bouncing down the stairs. Something was definitely different about her. She seemed a bit more reserved, a bit more confident, a bit more sophisticated.

"Hello, Jacob. It's so nice to see you again. I hope the trip went well."

"Rachel, you look beautiful. Yes, it's always so nice to see you as well."

So much for small talk. The banter continued this way for a short time but seemed an eternity. Finally, Louis, in his boisterous voice, broke the formality of the situation when he brought out a bottle of fine whiskey and poured a shot for each of them.

"It's time to relax and enjoy ourselves with a light drink and some good food."

Louis had his help take over the diner/gas station for the rest of the evening, and let Jacob know that he had made a reservation at a nearby restaurant that he thought Jacob would like. Rachel's mom excused herself for the evening. She was coming down with a nasty cold and wanted to remain in bed.

Jacob held the door open for Rachel while Louis got in the back seat. It turned out that the restaurant was just down the street toward the center of town, and they got there in no time. Every now and then, Jacob would glance over at Rachel and remember that the last time he drove a woman, it was Elizabeth in that space. Oddly enough, the memory did not cut to the core the way he thought it might. It was actually very refreshing to see Rachel there.

It was obvious that Louis had been a patron of the restaurant many times. The owner greeted him with a huge hug and a hearty handshake when he was introduced to Jacob.

"Hello, beautiful Rachel. It is so good to see you again. I have your favorite table waiting for you."

Jacob envisioned a dining room in Tuscany to look like this. It was certainly an Italian restaurant with a mandolin playing in the background. Casa Bella was actually the first Italian restaurant that Jacob had ever been to. Chianti bottles with wax from dripping candles were placed around the room and at the center of each table. Strings of gourds and grapes adorned the walls and ceilings.

The restaurant was fairly busy with smiling couples obviously enjoying themselves. The aroma of the garlic and tomatoes was abundant but made the place feel like one was eating in the kitchen. As Jacob viewed the patrons around him, he thought it seemed that plates were piled high with enough food for an army.

"Jacob, I have been bringing Rachel here since she was a baby. Sometimes I would call her Little Miss Pasta because she would be covered in orange sauce by the time the meal would be through. This was always our happy place, and I hope you will enjoy yourself here as well."

With that said, Emilio—the restaurant owner and head chef—came over and placed platters of meats, cheeses, and hot bread in the center of the table. A large bowl of orange gravy for dipping followed. This was a totally new experience for Jacob. Although he was not overly religious, he tended to eat Jewish style because that was what he was used to.

There was a certain order to how to put these delicacies together. Rachel and Louis could not keep from laughing as they watched Jacob dip the bread, followed by cheese and meat, and try to get it into his mouth without dripping all over himself. This was not kosher salami nor bologna. It was not corned beef nor pastrami. This was unlike anything he had ever experienced. Prosciutto, ham, sausage.

Oh, dear, he thought.

These incredible tastes were putting him over the edge. When he found out he was eating pork, he almost fell over. In the Jewish religion, it is sacrosanct to eat any part of a pig. One does not have to be religious to follow this rule. It is drilled into you when you are born. Once tasted, however, there was no going back. Jacob was having a buffet of fun.

To Jacob's surprise, Emilio returned to get their dinner orders.

"Wait a minute, there's more?"

"Jacob," Emilio said, as he poured him another glass of wine, "this was just an appetizer. I hope your appetite can hold a lot more."

By the time dinner was over, Jacob had consumed pasta, osso buco, eggplant, and salad. This was finished off with a large helping of tiramisu.

"I think I may have to walk back to Boston," Jacob said. "I don't ever remember eating this much at one sitting in my entire life."

When Jacob asked for the bill, he was told that it had already been taken care of.

"Louis, you must let me make this up to you. Next time, it's on me."

"Jacob, it does my heart good to know there will be a next time. You're on."

Emilio came back to the table to bid them all a good night. He was carrying a large paper bag that he handed to Jacob.

"Jacob, watching you enjoy every mouthful tonight brought tears to my eyes. Your expressions were heartwarming. I want you to bring some of this home so that when you heat it up and have it again, you will think of me and want to return. It was a pleasure meeting you, and I am happy that Rachel has such a nice friend. Next time, you will try the calamari."

Chapter 40

Being Cautious

Jacob dropped off Rachel and Louis at the diner but found he was reluctant to leave.

"Louis, how can I thank you enough for tonight? It was so much fun, and the food was so good. I don't think I'll eat again for a week."

With that, Louis said good night and went into the diner.

"Rachel, being with you makes me realize that there is still so much out there to see, to feel. I really like spending time with you and would like to see you again. Perhaps we can talk during the week and make plans to see each other again soon."

"Jacob, I also loved spending time with you, but I also understand how sensitive your situation is right now. Your future has been disrupted, and the easiest thing in the world would be for you to fall right back into a relationship. However, I have to protect myself. As much as I would like to keep seeing you, I think you need some time to mourn. Not enough time has gone by for you to know your own heart at this point. Let's give it some time. Take it slow. I'll be here for you, but be certain of the direction you are going in before you leap."

Jacob was stunned, to say the least. He knew she was right, and the last thing he wanted to do was hurt her; but Elizabeth had not been gone that long, and he wasn't really sure about where his feelings were landing.

"Rachel, I do understand where you are coming from, and you're right. The time we have spent together has been full of fun and adventure. I do care for you, but perhaps I must find the proper place to put Elizabeth in my life before I dive into another relationship. I hope you will be patient and give me some time to sort things out. I need to make sure of where I am going with this before I hurt either of us.

"As much as I would like to deny it, perhaps some time by myself is just what I need right now. Maybe a trip would give me some clarity. I care for you, Rachel. Really, I do. I never thought there would ever be anyone but Elizabeth in my life, but I must be certain of the road I am going down before I hurt anyone. Give me some time to come to terms with myself so that I can offer my whole heart to another."

With that, Jacob kissed Rachel lightly on the lips, gave her a tight embrace, and promised to stay in touch.

As soon as Jacob got home, he approached Heschel with an idea. "Heschel, I really need to spend some time alone to sort out my life from here on in. Up until the time Elizabeth died, I knew what path I was going on, but now I'm not sure. I am very fond of Rachel, but before I go any further with that relationship, I must first make certain that I am not using her as a safety net so I won't be alone.

"The thought of boarding a train going west is very attractive to me. It would give me some time to see the country, and I would be alone to maybe finally mourn Elizabeth and sort things out. It would mean you and Anthony would have to take up the slack once more and run the business without me. I won't take more than a month, maybe less, but I need to clear my confused mind. What do you think?"

"Jacob, the business is running well. Anthony has really caught on, and the customers seem to like him a lot. I promise, you can take whatever time you need. We'll still be here when you return. Just stay safe and stay in touch."

The following day, Jacob went to the railway station and mapped out a route that would take him on a southwest–northeast pattern. He would go through small towns, large cities, mountains, and deserts. He also knew that at any time he could cut the trip short and come home.

It was set. He would be leaving in three days. There was so much to do but no time to waste. The minute he bought his ticket, homesickness was already setting in.

Chapter 41

A Man on a Mission

Heschel had a difficult time trying to understand Jacob's sudden rush to be alone, to think things over. He knew for sure when he met Elizabeth, but his attraction to Rachel was different. In the end, it would probably be more stable, but it all came about so suddenly. He was hoping his big brother would find the answers to his questions on this solo train ride to wherever. Jacob did promise to call home every few days so that they would not worry, but his plans to call Rachel were not there. He wanted nothing to cloud his mind.

In three days' time, Jacob boarded the Boston-to-New York train. In New York, he would board a Pennsylvania Railroad train going west. He thought about Elizabeth's family and how different his was from hers. He wanted a life filled with love and devotion. He wanted to care for someone and to have them care as much for him. He didn't care so much about the material things in life but still wanted to be able to have enough to provide for a family. This was quite a rude awakening for a poor chicken farmer's son from Eastern Europe.

The strangest part of all this was that until he stopped thinking of himself as a poor chicken farmer's son, his demons would never be gone. Until he confronted Max, he would never be free. He hated, no, *despised* the thought of ever facing Max and Esther again, but he knew that until he unleashed all his hatred and disappointment on them he could never move on.

He had not been on the train very long when this realization came to him. All right, one problem solved. The train would only be stopped in New York with enough time to change to the train going west. For this he was grateful, because he could not have brought himself to disembark there. Of course, he had a sleeper cabin, and felt somewhat privileged to have it.

It was not long after that he put his head down and fell into a deep sleep. It was not a fitful sleep, however; he dreamt of demons and riots in his comfortable and safe place. He would awake in a cold sweat with the realization, that even though this was his dream he had lived it. More and more, he began to realize that his demons had to disembark during this trip.

The first leg on his trip was Philadelphia and then through Washington, DC. They then stopped in Baltimore, Maryland.

In Maryland, the patrons were allowed to disembark for two hours to tour the port. Jacob did not follow the Jewish doctrines of being kosher but had never had shellfish before. Going against everything he believed and held sacred, he dove right in and tasted the most wonderful thing he had ever had in his life.

How, he asked himself, *could this be a sin?*

The crab cake was mostly sweet crab with a smattering of bread crumbs. He dipped the crab cake into a tangy sauce, and Jacob thought he had died and gone to heaven. The first thing he thought of was if Rachel would enjoy this as much as he did.

Rachel. Not Elizabeth but *Rachel* was his first thought.

What to make of this? At any rate, Jacob was going to finish his incredible crab cake and move on. The heavy weight that had been hanging over him for so many months was beginning to leave, and it had only been day 2.

The following day, the train ventured through Virginia. The foothills of the mountains were so beautiful that Jacob almost cried.

What a wonderful country this is. Every part of this land has its own personality. I should love to share these sights with Rachel.

Once again, it was Rachel taking the space that was originally reserved for Elizabeth, and at once, he was homesick.

It has not been long enough to know my mind, he thought. *First, I must learn to be happy to be alone before I can offer myself up to anyone, before I can be a man.*

Unknown to Jacob at this time, the trip was the best thing he could have done for himself.

That night, Jacob fell asleep to the *click-clack-clicking* of the train tracks. This was reminiscent of the time he and Heschel had taken the train from New York to Boston. This time though, the rhythm of the tracks was comforting, and he fell into a sound sleep.

When the train stopped in Columbus, Ohio, to pick up more passengers, Jacob decided to get off to spend a couple of days there and explore the city.

Columbus, being the capital of Ohio, was a booming city. Lots of buildings and people bustling around. He checked with the conductor and had his ticket adjusted to ensure he would be able to embark on the train coming through in two days' time. He grabbed his luggage and approached the desk inside the train station.

"Excuse me. I am looking to stay in a hotel for the next two days and was wondering if you could suggest something decent."

"If you have never been to Columbus before, allow me to suggest the Great Southern Fireproof Hotel and Opera House. It may be slightly more expensive than other places, but the experience of being there is something you will never forget."

With that suggestion, arrangements were made for Jacob to taxi over. The minute he stepped into the lobby, he knew he had made the right choice.

I can't wait to bring Rachel here to see this.

Once again, his thoughts ran to Rachel.

The lobby was two stories high of marble. The hotel was fully electric, which was really ahead of its time, and the brightness in the lobby overtook him. As it said in its description, the hotel was fully fireproof. One of the other features was the Great Southern Theater that was attached. Nightly performances assured their guests that they would never be bored.

Jacob walked up to the registration desk and made sure they would have a room for him. It was fortunate that they did have an availability. At this point, he would have been disappointed to have to find somewhere else. This place was grand. Definitely a far cry from Shlomo's rooming house. Nevertheless, Jacob paid for two nights' stay in advance.

When he opened the door to his room, his surprise was almost gleeful. The room was as grand as the lobby, with its own bathroom.

Yes, he thought to himself. *I have worked hard and endured much. I have never splurged on anything for myself until now, and I will allow myself to enjoy this city.*

It was now late afternoon, and Jacob spent the time resting in his room reading the local newspaper. He found out that there was a river going around the city, the Scioto River, and he could get a ticket to take a river boat ride the next day.

That night, he dined in the hotel dining room. The dining room was packed with apparently happy couples and some families. He observed everything and only missed home more. After an incredible dinner, exhaustion set in. Tomorrow he would explore the city and take in a performance at the Great Southern Theater.

By the time he got back to his room, he barely made it to change into his nightclothes and go to sleep. Again, he slept peacefully. No demons.

Jacob awoke early the next morning and once again made his way into the main dining room. The coffee was piping hot and the best he had ever had. This hotel raised the bar for what he probably would be able to afford again. Everything was done to perfection.

After breakfast, Jacob walked around the city. It wasn't New York, but it was bustling with people and cars. So many automobiles. Horns were honking, and pickup trucks were lining the roads. When Jacob got to one of the docks, he inquired about a ticket for a river ride around the city. Fortunately, there was a tour leaving in an hour.

The small ferry was full of friendly people. Everyone spoke to him with questions about where he was from, how did he happen to be here in Columbus, etc. He didn't think of them as nosy. They were just friendly people who were interested in knowing him. Jacob did tend to be on the shy side, but most people found this endearing.

Once again, his thoughts went to Rachel. How much fun this would be with her alongside. All of a sudden, he heard gasps coming from his fellow travelers. They were passing an enormous mound of what appeared to be dirt.

The announcer on the ferry was explaining what this mound actually was. It was called the Adena Mound and was dated back to the era of Plato. This was thousands of years ago. It was actually a mound of clay containing charred wood and was believed to have been a sacrificial altar. The mound was unearthed over a period of time by purely accidental means. It never occurred to Jacob that there would be any antiquities in America, and he found this fascinating. One more thing to study about.

When the tour was over, Jacob returned to the hotel and made arrangements to go to theater that night. Before he did that, he stopped at the train station and traded his ticket for a new one going back east.

He didn't need any more time to make up his mind. Elizabeth would never be forgotten, but Rachel held a special place in his heart, and he knew he wanted to get back to her as soon as possible. He sent a telegraph to Heschel to let him know he would be returning home in a few days and could not wait to regain his old life. Yes, this trip did exactly what it was supposed to do. It cemented his feelings for Rachel, and he could not wait to let her know.

That night, Jacob saw a revival of a recent vaudeville show at the Great Southern Theater in back of the hotel. He felt a new sense of lightness now that he had made up his mind, and was able to sit back and thoroughly enjoy the show.

The next morning, Jacob awoke with a new bounce in his step and made his way to the train station. As soon as he boarded the train going east, he relaxed and took in the sights going back home.

Chapter 42

Home Again

In two days' time, Jacob arrived in New York City and boarded the train to Boston. This was a more direct route than the one he had taken when first arriving in this country. As soon as he arrived back in his apartment, he called Rachel to let her know he would be coming to see her the following weekend.

Heschel came home shortly after Jacob's arrival, and the excitement of being together again was heartfelt.

"Jacob, you must fill me in on everything. So much has gone on in the week since you have been gone, and I will fill you in as soon as you tell me about your adventure."

Jacob was glowing as he regaled Heschel with every minute of his trip ending in Ohio. Heschel was surprised that Jacob had ended his trip there, but was not as surprised at the conclusion he had come to. He was so happy for his brother. Jacob was back, but more importantly, Jacob had come to some decisions that were good for all.

"Heschel, please tell me what has been going on in my absence."

"Well, Jacob, no sooner had you left than Anthony came into the shop very excited. A wonderful storefront in the North End was becoming available, and Anthony wants to partner with us in opening a second shop. This one would concentrate more on the refinishing aspect of furniture, but the shop we have now would be strictly upholstery. We would then be bringing in the population of the North End of Boston, which would be huge. What do you think?

Of course, a decision this big would never be made without you, so for that, I am so happy you are back."

"Heschel, this sounds like a great idea. I never considered expanding our business, but Anthony is young, with a good sense of business. Also, the customers really like him, and he is well-known around his neighborhood. I say let's go for it."

With that, Heschel embraced Jacob, and the two men toasted to what would hopefully be a bright and successful future. Life was good.

The following day, Anthony brought Jacob to see the store. It was positioned right in the center of Faneuil Hall. This was one of the busiest areas in the city. Faneuil Hall was home to many merchants, fishermen, and meat and produce growers. Their little shop would not go unnoticed with so many people flocking around.

Jacob could feel the excitement growing. "Let's sign the lease agreement before it is gone."

He felt that no matter what the rent was, it would pay for itself tenfold. It would also bring business into their other shop. Expansion in business was happening, and expansion in his private life with Rachel seemed to be growing as well.

The only doubt in his mind was whether or not he would actually go to see Max. The very thought of it brought him down.

When Jacob got back to the shop with Anthony, they shared their news with Heschel and quickly called the landlord of the storefront. Thankfully, it was still available, and the landlord let them know that he would do whatever it took to get the store in move-in condition. There was equipment to buy, and they would have to secure a bank loan for that. Jacob had a wonderful reputation for always paying his creditors on time. Securing a loan would not be a problem.

One matter was conclusive, but there was the nagging matter of Max and Esther.

Chapter 43

Familiar Faces

Jacob was resigned to the fact that he would have to see Max and Esther, but he also had to spend some time with Rachel. He was not—maybe never—going to introduce her to them. With everything going on in his life right now, he really did not have any place to turn.

Rachel was arriving this Friday on the 9:00 a.m. train from Connecticut, but Jacob would be at the train station with bated breath until he saw her. As soon as she disembarked, he knew he had made the right decision. He was so happy to see her and she him.

"Rachel, I feel as though I have been to the moon and back. So much time has passed, but I could not wait to see you again. Thank you for coming in. How is your father and the diner?"

"Jacob, the traffic has become so busy going by the gas station and the diner so busy on top of that. I think we have to hire more people. Actually, my father has had several offers to buy the property, and he just may sell it. He's tired and does not want this to become my sole responsibility."

Jacob took this as a sign to make a bold move. "Rachel, I took a trip to clear my mind, but all I could think of was you. Can we see more of each other and see where it takes us?"

Rachel could not believe her ears. This was, after all, what she wanted. "Yes, Jacob. Take as much time as you need. I will be here."

Jacob felt as though God had given him a second chance. It had not been that long since Elizabeth was gone, but Rachel was perfect in his life. He could not have been happier. Still, he mourned Elizabeth by putting flowers on her grave and saying Yiscah on Friday nights. This was the mourner's kaddish. He planned to say it for a year in honor of her.

Rachel was another matter. Jacob was more enthralled as days went by. His love for her was true but not with any stipulations. He just enjoyed her company and wanted it to be more. So it was by the late winter of 1929 when Jacob proposed marriage. The two stores were doing a booming business, and he could not have thought of anyone whom he could care for more. The decision was made. June 29 would be their wedding date.

It had been two years since Elizabeth's death, and Jacob decided it was time to visit Elizabeth's family in New York. He had stayed in touch with them by phone and letter but had not been back to see them. He also wanted to touch base with Shlomo and Frank to let them know what had been going on in his life. It was now April 1929, and the Passover holiday was approaching. Jacob called Mr. Levy and made arrangements to attend the first seder with his family. He hoped they would be happy for him.

Jacob contacted Shlomo and made arrangements to spend the following Friday night with him. The first seder was on Friday night, April 26, and he would spend the first seder with Elizabeth's family and then head over to spend the night with Shlomo. On his way home on Saturday, he would stop in Connecticut and have the second seder with Rachel and her family. Jacob had stayed in touch with Frank but had not been back to work in his shop since Elizabeth had died. Visiting him would have to wait.

On April 26, Jacob drove to New York, and the reunion with Mr. Levy was heartwarming. He had become like family to him but had to break the news about Rachel gingerly. To his surprise, Mr. Levy was ecstatic for him. He was never under the impression that Jacob would spend the rest of his life alone, and after he heard how Jacob had met Rachel to begin with, he was delighted.

"Jacob, next time you come here, please bring your fiancée with you. I'm certain the rest of the family will be equally as thrilled."

The two men walked over to Aunt Evelyn's house, and the relief on Jacob's face was obvious. For whatever reason, he was so hesitant to tell everyone. As predicted, they were all so happy for him. It turned out to be the best evening he had in a long time. It had also been a very long time since he celebrated a proper Passover.

After the meal was over, and all hugs and kisses with promises to be back soon had ended, Jacob headed to Shlomo's.

"Hello, my old friend." Shlomo greeted Jacob the way a long-lost brother would greet his sibling. "Let's get out the schnapps while you fill me in on what you have been doing since I last saw you."

Jacob told Shlomo everything, and once again, Jacob was overcome with joy at the happiness this man felt for him. Jacob never met anyone he did not touch. The only dark spot in his entire life was his own father. This still was like a dark cloud hovering over him, and he was determined to deal with it before his wedding. The thoughts relating to that horrible incident in Poland were becoming fainter and fainter as he got older. It had become like a bad dream. For that, he was grateful.

"Shlomo, my friend, I have been blessed a second time and am happier than I deserve. How about you? Is there any room in your life to find a bride?"

"Jacob, I have had several loves in my life but none that I would want to spend the rest of my life with. You have definitely been blessed, and I am so happy for you. Perhaps the girl of my dreams is walking down the street right now."

With that, the two men embraced like old souls. Jacob bid Shlomo a good night and went to bed. The following day, he would stop and celebrate Passover with Rachel and her family.

These sweet thoughts were on Jacob's mind as he slumbered into a deep and comforting sleep.

Chapter 44

An Unforeseen Loss

The following morning, Jacob sped through a hearty breakfast and took off for Connecticut. He felt as if he were walking on clouds. What a difference from a year ago, when he thought he would never smile again.

The drive through Connecticut was beautiful. Spring was here, and the trees were just beginning to show their buds. It was a glorious day. Soon he would see Rachel.

Jacob finally drove up to the diner, and Rachel and Louis came running out. The excitement of being together for the first time to celebrate Passover was very meaningful to them all.

"Come on in, Jacob," said Louis. "You must be tired from your trip."

Rachel sat him down and poured him a nice hot cup of tea. "Jacob, Heschel has called and asked you to call him when you got here."

"That seems strange. I wonder what it can be about. Maybe something has happened at the store?"

When Jacob finally got around to calling Heschel, he could not believe what he was being told.

"Jacob, Elizabeth's aunt Evelyn called this morning to let you know that Mr. Levy passed away in his sleep last night. It was very sudden. She told me that he had never fully recovered from Elizabeth's death and spoke often of wanting to join her. She wanted to make certain that you knew before you got back to Boston because the funeral will be first thing Monday morning."

Typically, people who follow the Jewish religion would bury the deceased within twenty-four hours of their death. The first two days of Passover are considered to be holy; therefore, no funeral could take place until it is over. The second day of Passover happened to fall on a Sunday, so the funeral would have to take place on Monday morning.

Jacob had to first wrap his mind around the fact that he had just been with Mr. Levy last night, and now he knew he would never see him again.

"Rachel, would it be all right if I stayed here until Monday morning?"

"Of course, Jacob. It would be silly for you to drive all the way back to Boston just to turn around and drive all the way back to New York for the funeral. This is becoming your home too, and you can stay for as long as you need. I am truly sorry for your loss."

Rachel knew how much Mr. Levy meant to Jacob. She showed Jacob to his room so that he could rest awhile and absorb this sudden event. Rachel went down to the kitchen, where her mother was preparing the Passover meal. Jacob had met Rachel's mother briefly each time he came to Connecticut but had never spent much time in her company.

Rachel always spoke kindly of her mother. Her name was Janice, and she was a portly, sweet, but quiet woman. Louis was the more outgoing of the two. Tonight, Jacob would have time to get to know Janice.

In many respects on initial appearances, she seemed to be the kind of woman his own mother, Sarah, was. Her priority was her home, her children and tending to all that needed to be done for Louis and Rachel.

As soon as sundown approached, the seder began. Jacob's heart was so heavy. He wanted to join in with the singing and reading of the Haggadah (Passover prayer book), but he couldn't shake the black cloud hanging over his head. Last night at this exact time, he had sat around Aunt Evelyn's seder table drinking wine, breaking the matzos, and enjoying the holiday. What a difference twenty-four hours could make.

Feeling that this was not being fair to Rachel and her family, he tried as much as possible to act joyful and join in with the celebration. If truth be told, he couldn't wait to be alone with his thoughts and sadness.

Besides Rachel, Louis, and her mother, several of their neighbors joined them for what turned out to be a joyful evening of food, wine, and singing. Jacob felt so fortunate to have fallen into two families with basically the same values. He was shown more love and admiration than ever before in his life. Yet this cloud still hung.

The following day, Rachel showed Jacob around the Connecticut countryside. They walked and talked for several hours and got to know each other more and more. The more Jacob found out about Rachel, the more he became enamored of her. Her mother, who up until now had been a stranger, took him in and treated him as a son. The time went quickly. Before he knew it, it was Monday morning, and he headed back to New York City.

It was with a heavy heart that Jacob entered the funeral home and sat with Aunt Evelyn and the rest of the family. Mr. Levy's death had been such a shock to everyone, but the family felt that he had died from a broken heart after Elizabeth's death. He had just lost his will to live.

After the burial, the family went back to Aunt Evelyn's house to begin the week of mourning. Jacob felt he could only stay a short time. In the end, this was not his real family, and with Mr. Levy now gone, he would most likely not be returning.

As he was leaving, he felt it had become apparent to everyone that this would probably be goodbye, but nonetheless, he promised to stay in touch.

Jacob got in his car and headed straight for home. He was not even going to stop to see Rachel on his way. He was anxious to get back to Heschel, work, and his normal way of life. He had a wedding to look forward to and an apartment to lease. On top of that, he had a honeymoon to plan.

Chapter 45

Max Is Back

Jacob arrived home in the early evening and was surprised to find Ariel there with Heschel. He was very fond of her and was happy that she put a huge smile on Heschel's face, but he really wanted some alone time with Heschel.

Sensing this, Heschel told Ariel to get her wrap and that he would take her home. Tomorrow was a workday.

By the time Jacob had unpacked and poured himself a tall whiskey, Heschel returned. "My brother, I have been so concerned for you. How are you doing?"

Jacob related the events of the past several days and let Heschel know how happy he was to be home. "Heschel, I think I have to try to make amends with Max in order to go on peacefully in my own life. I will never love him as a son, but the hatred is burning inside of me, and I must let it go."

"Jacob, I am so happy to hear you say that. Yes, Max is an evil man, but he's still our father. If you can let him into your life, even a little bit, it will make your life easier. To tell you the truth, it will make *my* life easier as well.

"I have been reluctant to bring Ariel over to meet them, but if we can all go together, it will be less stressful. I have no love for that family either, but at the end of life, we have to be able to look back and know that we have honored our father. God will take care of the rest."

As weary as Jacob was, he realized the significance of what Heschel was saying. Max would get his just desserts, but it would be from a force much greater than them. "All right. The three of us can go on Sunday if you wish to bring Ariel, but I am not so inclined to bring Rachel just yet. Let's see how this goes. After that, I am not making any promises."

The week went quickly. Jacob called Rachel every evening to say good night, and she regaled him with stories of all the plans her cousins and aunts were making for her engagement. Jacob still felt absolutely certain that he was making the right decision. He let her know that he would be seeing Max the following Sunday, and her response was encouraging.

"Jacob, he is still your father, and it would make me so happy if you could make amends with him."

"Rachel, I am not promising anything. A leopard does not change its spots. My father does not have a bit of love or compassion in his bones. However, yes, I will try to keep an open mind, but at the first sign of disrespect to me or to Heschel, I will fly out of there."

Sunday morning rolled around, and Jacob and Heschel headed to Millis. As habit would have it, they stopped at their favorite roadside diner for breakfast on the way. The coffee was steaming hot, and procrastinating over extra cups came easy. This was not a trip they were looking forward to. Heschel had decided that this would not be the appropriate time to bring Ariel, so it was just the two of them. After two hours and several cups, they decided it was time to hit the road. After all, how bad could it actually be?

When little David saw the car pull up the path to the house, he came running out to greet the boys. "Heschel, Jacob, I am so happy to see you."

Jacob could not believe how much David had grown. Even though David was his half-brother, he knew he could not hold him responsible for his parents. At this point, he was just a little boy born into a tough family.

David grabbed both men's hands and ushered them into the house. Max was seated in his wheelchair, and Esther was in the kitchen.

"Hello, Max."

"Since when do you address me as though I were not your father? Strangers call me Max. I expect my sons to refer to me with more respect."

With that said, the blood was already boiling in Jacob's body, but in essence, Max was not wrong.

"Hello, Papa," said Jacob.

"Hello, Papa" came next from Heschel.

"Hello, everyone" came from David, sort of killing the tension in the room.

Next came Esther. "Hello, boys. I'm delighted to see you. It's been too long."

"Esther, I'll be honest," Jacob said. "Neither Heschel nor I have ever felt welcomed here. My father has never really been a father to either one of us. I have learned what a loving family looks like now, and if that is not what I can expect from either of you, then don't expect me to address you in loving terms.

"I'm getting married in the late spring, and I would like you to all be there, but if you cannot appear to be happy for me, then I would rather you stayed home. I did not come here to say such unpleasant things, but it's hard to keep my feeling inside when there is so much history between us that has gone unsaid."

Heschel could not believe what he was hearing. Jacob had certainly grown into an independent man to be admired.

Max looked at both boys and said, "Jacob, I have done my best as a father. The times did not call for coddling, and therefore, I did not coddle you. I sent you away because I had no choice, and it seems that it only helped you grow into a wise adult. I have no regrets."

"You have no idea what suffering I have gone through because of your lack of caring. I did not need to be coddled, but I did need to know that I was not thrust into the world without even a thought to how either of us would live.

"When we finally came to America, you tossed me out to the streets again without even a care in the world. That is not how a father should act, especially when I had no other parent to guide me. No, Max, you do not deserve to be called Papa, at least not by me.

"I am getting married in June, and you, Esther, and David will still be invited. However, you will be my guests. You have never treated me as a family member, and I shall not consider you one ever again.

"David, I am sorry that you had to witness this. I will always be your big brother, and you can always come to me, but I will not be back on Sundays to visit. I've said my piece."

"You are an ungrateful son. I have done everything for you. I brought you to America to give you a good life, and it seems to have worked out well."

"No, Max. You brought me to America, but you have done nothing to give me a good life. Through happenstance, I have made the most of what I have and what I have learned. You had nothing to do with it. I really thought that we could put all this behind us, but if you cannot take any responsibility for your actions, then I must move on. Heschel may be more forgiving than me, and I would never hold that against him. I have a new family now that shows me love and devotion, and that is where I will place my heart."

With that, Jacob grabbed little David and gave him a big bear hug.

"Don't forget, little brother," he whispered. "I will always be here for you. Nothing I have said will ever be directed at you.

"Come, Heschel, I must get back. There is much to do. I will be waiting in the car."

For the second time in his life, Jacob had stood up to Max, and the burden of his father was lifted from his being. He felt a final sigh of relief. Yes, he would actually invite them to his wedding, but he would bet his life on it that they would not come. All he could think of was Rachel, and those thoughts put a smile on his face.

The ride home was spent in silence. Heschel was not quite sure of how he felt about the events of the day. He always felt that Jacob had endured something awful while at Jordanna's, but Jacob never spoke of it. At one point, something suddenly changed, and Jacob had become more sullen, more serious. Perhaps that was the one thing he was referring to when he mentioned his suffering.

Chapter 46

The Next Chapter

April seemed to fly by. By the time June came around, all plans for the wedding were set. The wedding would take place in Connecticut, with the reception at the synagogue they would be getting married in. Rachel and her mother had taken care of all the arrangements. When the invitations went out, Jacob included Shlomo, Frank, and Saul. Of course, Anthony was also invited along with his parents, who were constantly sending food to work. Until Jacob met Rachel, he had never experienced Italian cooking. Now he couldn't get enough of Anthony's mother's incredible dishes. Anthony was amazing at what he did, and the customers really liked him. Both shops were doing well.

The wedding was fast approaching, and Jacob had decided to take his bride to a hotel in New Hampshire for a week. It was 1929, and a girl's virginity was considered sacred in most circles. Jacob and Rachel had never been intimate. In fact, to begin with, Jacob had never been intimate with a woman up until now, but he had gotten so close to Rachel in the past few months that he knew the intimacy would just come naturally.

Jacob found a perfect apartment in the west end of Boston. It was the first floor of a brownstone, and the neighbors were either young newlyweds or families with young children. It was a perfect environment to bring Rachel home to. He was convinced that she would have lots of company during her coffee klatches. Rachel was coming up the following weekend with her parents to see the apartment and begin to furnish it.

At the same time, Heschel and Ariel were moving along in what was turning into a serious relationship. Jacob was certain that his betrothal would soon follow.

Last weekend, Rachel's mother made a lavish engagement party for Rachel and Jacob. This was where he got to meet the entire family. Jacob had never considered Rachel to have a large family because she lived with her parents in somewhat of an isolated part of Connecticut. He was pleasantly surprised to see how large her family actually was. Some of her relatives had come over from Eastern Europe, but many were born in America.

It was at this party that Jacob really felt his isolation from whatever family he had and the family he never even knew about. Surely, his parents had family who had immigrated to America as well. His father never spoke of it, and he never asked.

Heschel and Ariel came in for the party, and Jacob was elated to see how Ariel and Rachel got along. This would be the family he would build on.

The next few weeks flew by. Suddenly, the date for the wedding was approaching. In the Jewish religion, it is customary for a bride to attend a mikvah before the wedding. It is a private but religious cleansing of the body before the ceremony.

Rachel was not particularly religious, and the thought of doing this made her very uncomfortable. She would have to be stripped naked and expose herself to the person performing the cleansing. It is done in a sanctuary reserved for this purpose only.

Rachel approached Jacob about her apprehensions regarding this service. To her amazement, he agreed wholeheartedly with her feelings. Who was he to judge anything pertaining to a religious ceremony? After all, he was brought up in a brothel. She felt so relieved that this did not matter to him and was reminded once again why she loved him so much.

Chapter 47

The Wedding

June 29, 1929, was a perfect spring day. The sun was shining, and the synagogue was filled with flowers and candles. Seventy-five guests, wearing their finest, were seated in the chapel.

Heschel and the rabbi accompanied Jacob down the aisle before the bridesmaids strolled down. Ariel was actually Rachel's maid of honor, even though they had not known each other all that long. It was a relationship that was blossoming into sisterhood.

Then the music stopped, and a rendition of "Here Comes the Bride" began on a beautiful but soft flute. Jacob's heart was beating a mile a minute as he watched with bated breath his beautiful bride, flanked on either side by her parents, walk toward him. He felt happiness he could never have imagined.

Louis lifted Rachel's veil, kissed her on the cheek, and shook Jacob's hand as he handed him is bride. "Take good care of her, my son."

It was as poignant as could be, and Jacob could not believe that this was his wedding and this was his bride.

The ceremony ended, the glass was broken, and Jacob wrapped his arms around his bride and kissed her softly and lovingly.

"Mazel tov!" rang out in the shul, and Rachel walked back down the aisle as Mr. and Mrs. Jacob Kalinsky. Everyone was joyful.

They paraded into the function hall and greeted their guests. Heschel and Ariel were so emotional, and at the same time, Heschel felt sad that Max did not attend. He was torn with what to do when his time came. He was not as strong as Jacob. These thoughts, however, could wait until tomorrow.

The rest of the evening comprised of dancing, eating, drinking, and just joyful celebration. At the end of the evening, Rachel threw her bouquet, and, of course, Ariel caught it. The same went for Jacob's throw of the garter; of course, Heschel caught it.

As Jacob and Rachel left for their honeymoon, tears ran down Rachel's cheeks.

"My sweetheart, what is wrong?" Jacob asked.

"Nothing, Jacob. Everything is right. I am crying for the happiness I am feeling right now."

"You have my undying love and devotion." Jacob paused, looked at his bride, and said, "I am a lucky man."

Never before in his life had he ever truly felt that way.

"Now let's begin our honeymoon, and think of nothing but being cared for and catered to for the next week. I truly love you, Rachel."

That evening, they arrived at their destination and were greeted by the hotel staff.

"Hello, Mr. and Mrs. Kalinsky. We have the honeymoon suite prepared and waiting for you."

Rachel could not help but blush uncontrollably. Jacob looked at her and laughed. It was about to be a new experience for both.

The following morning, Rachel awoke and watched Jacob as he slept. She felt so much love for him. Last night was as natural as could be, and the two of them finally admitted to being previously nervous. But as they fell into the arms of each other, the rest came naturally. Their lovemaking was tender and brought them even closer than they ever could have imagined. Finally, being spent from the events of a very long day, they fell asleep, with Rachel nestled on Jacob's shoulder. Although it was a new experience for each of them, it seemed like they had been this way forever.

Finally, Jacob woke up and saw Rachel staring down at him smiling. "Good morning, my love. Have you been up long?"

"I could stay here watching you sleep all day. It is all so surreal to me in a wonderful way, but now I need my morning coffee. Let's go to breakfast."

When Jacob and Rachel entered the dining room, all eyes seemed to knowingly be on them. Once again, Rachel could not help but blush in embarrassment. Jacob could not help but laugh. The dining room was filled with lots of young couples and families. The energy was palpable. It was going to prove to be a wonderful day with lots of activities, or if one desired, it could be a wonderful day to sit on the veranda to just relax or read.

The week seemed to fly by. The Fourth of July celebration was like nothing either had ever experienced before. Between the special barbecues, the decorations, and entertainment, the honeymoon could not have been more perfect. Of course, the evening was capped off with a great fireworks display. The best part was that they still had two more days of being there before getting back to reality.

Jacob was thrilled as was Rachel. They met many young couples who were also staying at the resort, but for the most part, they were happy to be alone.

Conversation never seemed to be difficult. Jacob opened up to Rachel more than he had ever opened up to anyone. His deep dark secret, however, remained hidden. The shame he felt over that incident never left, even if it remained buried in the recesses of his mind. He was only fifteen years old when he was attacked in his sleep, and no one would ever blame him, but it was not in his nature to share this with anyone.

The morning of July 6, they bid goodbye to the staff with a promise to return. The week was wonderful, but Rachel could not wait to begin to be a housewife in her own home whose job was to take care of her loving husband. At the same time, Jacob was anxious to get back to work and spend the rest of his life with Rachel.

Chapter 48

A New Life

As Jacob opened the door to their new apartment, he swept Rachel up in his arms and carried her over the threshold. She and her mother had done a great job decorating the apartment. It was warm and inviting. Rachel could not wait to attack the kitchen and make her first meal as Mrs. Kalinsky.

Soon after they arrived, Karla, their pretty and energetic downstairs neighbor, arrived with baskets of cakes and cookies. Jacob had done a great job in securing this apartment. Rachel had met some of the neighbors while she was fixing up the place, and they all seemed to be warm and accepting. Being a newlywed would be nice, she thought. The apartment was spotless, and she could not stop admiring the great job she and her mother had done in fixing it up. Jacob was pleased, which made her even happier.

Jacob brought all the luggage into the apartment and asked Rachel if she would mind him leaving for a while to check into the shop and say hi to Heschel. She, of course, did not mind at all. In fact, she was happy to have this time alone to unpack and get things organized.

The first thing she had to do, however, was call her parents and let them know how wonderful the honeymoon had been. She was over the moon in love with Jacob and knew the feeling was reciprocal.

Jacob rushed over to his shop, where he found Heschel in deep conversation with a customer.

"Jacob!" he shouted as soon as he saw him come through the door. He excused himself from the customer with a promise to get right back to her. "How are you? How is married life?"

With that, they both had a good laugh. After all, it had only been a week.

"Let me finish up with this lovely lady, and we'll close shop early and go over to see Anthony."

Heschel continued his conversation with the customer for quite a while longer. The furrows in his forehead seemed to go from deep lines to small creases. Finally, they seemed to be done. They shook hands and promised to be in touch within a week. By now, Jacob was curious about who this smartly dressed woman could be.

Heschel immediately ran to the front door and put up the Closed sign.

"Heschel, what in the world is going on? Who is this person that had you so deep in conversation?"

"Jacob, I have a wonderful welcome-home gift for you. That woman is Mrs. Hermione Steele of the Steele Resorts. She is building a large hotel in Boston and would like us to make all the furniture for the common areas. She said after asking around, our name kept coming up as the most respected and talented people in the furniture industry in Boston.

"Jacob, do you know what this means? This kind of work can put us over the top into a whole new industry. We will, of course, have to expand and hire more people, but this could be the beginning of reaching our goals to have the kind of future we always dreamed of."

"Slow down. We would definitely have to have a proper contract and bank financing to undergo such a large project. Have you even seen plans for this project?"

"When she first came in, she showed me some preliminary plans and left them with me to go over with our lawyer and banker. Of course, they look like Greek to me, but I know that you and Anthony will be able to get a good sense of what needs to be done by looking them over. Let's go over to Anthony's shop. I'm sure he'll be delighted to see you, and we can talk about this project with him. I'm so glad to see you. The wedding was wonderful, and Ariel cannot wait to see Rachel."

"I hope you don't wait too long to make an honest woman out of her. After all, the sooner you put a ring on her finger, the sooner we can start expanding our family together."

As they left the shop, Jacob could not help but feel like the luckiest man alive. Everything was falling into place. He could not wait to get home to see Rachel.

Anthony was so excited to see Jacob and wanted to know all the details about his honeymoon. Well, not *all* the details. The three men sat down and went over the plans for the new hotel and looked over all the common areas on paper.

Fortunately, Anthony had an eye for such things and was able to dissect the plans into seating arrangements and groupings of furniture. Certainly, it was something they could handle but not without more employees and a larger space. This would, they all agreed, also require funding from the bank.

They all decided that the first order of business would be to have a meeting with an attorney and then a sit-down meeting with Mrs. Steele and her associates to map out the direction they were to go in. So much had to be done before they could even begin this project. Up until this moment, they had only been small shop owners. It was easy to get ahead of themselves, but what did any of them really know about big business?

Having grown up in the north end of Boston, Anthony had lots of relatives nearby and could count on them to point them in the right direction. His uncle was very friendly with a lawyer whom he trusted. The first step was to set up a meeting with him to see what they had to do to protect themselves.

So it was that this partnership with Abe Cohen was established. Abe was a jolly middle-aged man who happened to be born into an academic family in Boston. He got his law degree at Harvard and was respected as a scholar as well as an attorney. There was little Abe did not seem to know about.

The first meeting with Abe was with the three young men look-ing to create a dynasty. Of course, Jacob was just back from his hon-eymoon and had not yet come down to earth. Abe took an imme-diate liking to these three craftsmen, and after an initial three-hour meeting, he mapped out a plan for what had to be done and how.

First came the question of his retainer. Getting him his ini-tial retainer would not be a problem, but expenses after that would need backing. Abe pointed the boys to a banker who would be able to secure them financing. He did not see that as a problem due to their pristine credit history. Before this could be accomplished, they needed to set up a meeting with the group from Steele Resorts and get a contract written up. They needed to know time line, budget, quantities, unknown problems arising, etc. They had to be sure to be covered for any situation.

When their initial meeting with Abe was over, the three of them let out a sigh of relief. In their haste, they had overlooked so many things that could go wrong, but now felt that they were in the right hands and would be headed in the right direction.

That night, Jacob and Heschel took Rachel and Ariel to a very exclusive restaurant to celebrate what they perceived to be the begin-ning of a great partnership. No one could have been more surprised than Jacob when Heschel got down on one knee and proposed to Ariel in the middle of the restaurant. He pulled a beautiful diamond ring from his jacket pocket and slipped it on Ariel's finger. Her sur-prise was palpable: YES! She could not contain her excitement.

The entire restaurant, which was filled with patrons, got up and cheered. What a night this was turning into. Rachel jumped up and hugged Ariel, who was to become the sister she never had. Jacob embraced Heschel as well. It was not even ten years ago that their lives were so different. As they say, "Only in America."

Heschel's relationship with Max was not like Jacob's. He wanted to introduce Ariel to Max, Esther, and David. So it was on the fol-lowing weekend he drove to Millis and visited them.

As soon as he introduced Ariel as his betrothed, Max became belligerent. "Why are you so fast to introduce us to your girlfriend when your brother has not even introduced us to his wife?"

"Papa, I came here with the most respect. My relationship with you is not the same. I was hoping for your blessing."

"Well, we are doing just fine without your weekly visits. I cannot just overlook the months we have gone without seeing either of you. Good luck to you and Ariel. I hope you have a good life, but obviously, it will be without us."

Totally humiliated, Heschel grabbed Ariel's hand and walked her out of the house.

Poor David came running after. "Please do not leave. He is out of his mind and cannot see reason."

Esther, on his footsteps, also came, begging Heschel to reconsider running out. This was to no avail. Max was a miserable man with no redeeming qualities, and Jacob had been right to write him out of his life.

At this point, Heschel would as well. Ariel was his life now, and he would continue to build on that. Max was to become a distant memory. His only compassion was for David.

Chapter 49

August 1929

Life was good. Funding for the new Steele Hotel came easy, and there were enough people looking for work to train in the business. The banks were more than happy to invest in anything involving Steele Management, so the brothers and Anthony had no problem getting financing. It just seemed to flow. Jacob and Company, the name they decided upon, was doing a fantastic business, had a great reputation, and thrived on being honest and timely. Heschel and Ariel were planning their wedding, along with Rachel's wonderful expertise. Life was good.

Labor Day weekend came, and the brothers brought their women to the beach for the day. Castle Island was a wonderful spot in Boston, and picnicking and beaching was nothing but carefree. Heschel had related his last encounter with Max, and although, he still felt pangs of regret, he recognized what a toxic environment it would be for his future. He and Jacob had each other, their partners, and good friends. What could go wrong?

Sadly, these would be the last carefree days for a while. September 6, 1929, the news of the day was the stock market crash. Neither brothers had investments in the stock market, but their financing, along with Steele's financing, had been with the banks. As the banks went under, so did Steele Resorts. Jacob and Company got caught in the crosshairs.

No one could have prepared themselves for the black Friday that was to follow. On September 6, 1929, the stock market plummeted. For most people who did not invest in the stock market, one would have thought twice about being detached from this fateful day. Neither Jacob nor Heschel were savvy about the stock market and, in fact, had never invested, so in their minds, this was to have no effect on them. This could not have been further from the truth.

Margin calls were placed and could not be met, the banks lost money, and loans were called in. If a loan could not be paid, overseers for the banks would foreclose on homes and businesses. This caused a ripple effect right down to Jacob and Company.

There had been no warning at how bad things could get so fast. Jacob's business had just taken out a loan that was being called back by the bank. Some of it had already been spent on rent, retainers, and goods. The Steele Resorts quickly went under, and by the beginning of 1930, they were in dire straits. They could not afford to pay back the bank, and the business was foreclosed on.

Heschel and Ariel had to put their wedding on hold, and Jacob had to start all over again. Their bright future was looking very dim. It didn't help that the rest of the world was suffering alongside them. They had worked so hard to be on the brink of achieving so much more.

Fortunately, Jacob and Rachel had saved enough money to carry them through paying the rent and putting food on the table. Rachel's parents had a business that pretty much ran itself and was necessary. Jacob's heart went out to Heschel, who wanted so badly to marry Ariel and begin their life together.

What was important was that Heschel and Ariel be together, and so a small wedding was had with very little pomp and circumstance. Ariel wore Rachel's wedding gown, and everyone pitched in with homemade food. By February, Ariel became Mrs. Heschel Kalinsky and moved into Heschel's apartment. The honeymoon would have to wait for a more prosperous time.

Jacob and Company had a new start. Jacob, Heschel, and Anthony were able to rent a small storefront in the west end of Boston and live off the meager business that would come in. People were poor, but some things still needed repair. Some of what they did was paid for on the bartering system. The three men would never get rich running their business this way, but the main thing was to survive at all costs. This world of despair would someday come to an end, and they would build their business back again.

Chapter 50

October 1934

The previous three years had gone by without incident. Business was slow; however, it seemed that the most sparse days were over. The patrons were starting to come back, and job security was growing.

Jacob and Company had endured the worst and had survived. Anthony was once again in his own small storefront in the north end, and Heschel and Jacob were upholstering and refurbishing furniture in their own shop. Rachel and Ariel could not have been closer if they were related by blood. Rachel was pregnant with their first child, and Ariel would be several months behind. The hope was that they would all be able to afford to move into larger apartments near each other so the children could grow up close.

On October 19, 1934, Rachel felt the first pangs of labor. She was a small woman with a huge belly. Her belly seemed to outweigh the rest of her body. As soon as labor began, Jacob rushed her into the hospital. They were so nervous that the entire staff began to shudder. There had been hundreds of nervous first-time parents passing these hallways before, but the blubbering of Jacob defied description. One could only laugh. Actually, not Rachel. She was in dire pain.

Upon inspection, the doctor rushed her into the operating room to prepare for a C-section. The baby was too large to pass through her birth canal. Once in the operating room, Rachel was given anesthesia, and when she awoke, she was holding a ten-and-a-half-pound baby boy in her arms. Exhausted but happy, she looked up at a beaming Jacob.

"Ten fingers, ten toes, two ears, two eyes, one nose, and one mouth. We have a perfect baby!" Jacob exclaimed.

Rachel's parents and brothers would be over the next day to see the newest addition to their family. Heschel and Ariel had spent the entire time with Jacob in the waiting room.

"Please, can we see him now?" pleaded Ariel.

"Yes, of course. He cannot wait to meet his aunt and uncle."

"He's huge!" proclaimed Heschel. "How did such a small woman produce such a large baby?"

Rachel and little Steven Jay left the hospital on day 6. Jacob had asked that the baby be named for his mother, Sarah, and Jordanna. So it was that Steven Jay Kalinsky came home. On day 8, the rabbi from the temple, along with a mohel, came to the Kalinsky apartment to perform the bris. Little Steven had his first taste of wine and barely cried during the quick service. The circumcision was brief, but the wine had a lasting effect, and Steven Jay spent the rest of the afternoon sound asleep while relatives and friends drank wine, ate, and celebrated this beautiful new life.

Steven was such a robust child that it was a shock to everyone when at eight weeks old he developed scarlet fever. Although a serum was in use to fight against this disease, it was not readily available, nor had it been used on an infant this young. Rachel and Steven had to lock themselves in quarantine until the fever passed.

This was the most unnerving part of Rachel's life. She could conquer anything as long as her child was safe. His fever would rise and fall daily. This was highly contagious, and Rachel was not allowed out of the room. Food had to be passed through the door, and she was not let out of the room for four weeks. The porta-potty became her bathroom, and a warm bowl of water with towels became her bath. Fortunately, her nursing was not affected, and Steven never lost his appetite.

After four weeks, the fever broke, and Steven had a full recovery. The scars of those four weeks, however, haunted Rachel as a mother for the rest of her life. She never quite got over the fear of losing a child.

February 14 may have been a day for lovers, but it was also the day Harrison Kalinsky came into the world. It was only a fitting Valentine's Day gift for Heschel from Ariel. Harrison came into this world weighing seven pounds and eight ounces. He was instantly deemed to be Steven's best friend.

This was probably one of the happiest times in Rachel's life. She and Jacob moved into a three-bedroom apartment, and Heschel and Ariel moved in right next door. Dorchester was a suburb of Boston but close enough to the downtown area that a streetcar ride was but a few minutes away from taking the babies for walks in the gardens of Boston.

Heschel, Jacob, and Anthony purchased a three-store front not far from home, and Jacob and Company was once again prospering. There was fear of a war breaking out overseas, but hopefully, the United States would not be dragged into it.

The war, however, did bring a lot of prosperity into the country as machinery, artillery, and boats were being built. Adolf Hitler was chancellor of Germany and was intent on conquering Europe. For now, Dorchester, Massachusetts, was so far removed from this terror, and a sense of harmony prevailed.

Chapter 51

November 1938

Like any other day, November 26, 1938, was a restful Sunday in the Kalinsky home. Rachel was puttering around the kitchen, still cleaning up from the massive Thanksgiving dinner she had prepared the Thursday before. Once again pregnant, and due at any time, she was nowhere near the size she had been with Steven. This had been a much more comfortable pregnancy.

Steven was following her around the kitchen, mimicking her every move. He was a delightful child, easygoing and bright. She could not believe how much love a mother could have for her child. Jacob was a doting father who never missed a Friday night of flowers for her and candy for Steven. Rachel's parents had sold the diner and moved to Boston. They were also doting grandparents who helped with Steven as often as Rachel would let them.

Now she was bursting with child ready to be born, when all of a sudden, a splash of water came from beneath her dress.

"OH NO!" she yelled. "Jacob, call my parents!"

Jacob took off like he was on fire and got Rachel to the hospital in record time. This time, however, the baby would not wait. There was no time for a C-section. Benjamin Leon Kalinsky would wait for no one.

By the time they entered the hospital and got Rachel into a gown, Benjamin was on his way to greet the world. Another boy. Another bris. Another mouth to feed.

The house was becoming a busy place with lots of noise, laundry, and crying. Rachel was in her element. Jacob was happy to have a place to return to every day. By the time he got home, the boys would be bathed and in their pajamas. Rachel and he could still enjoy a quiet meal together and discuss the problems of the day. Things overseas were becoming tenuous but still should not be involving the United States. At this rate, anyhow, neither Jacob nor Heschel would qualify to be drafted.

Not to be outdone by Rachel, Ariel soon followed with the birth of Samantha on December 18, 1938. As happy as Rachel was for Heschel and Ariel, she still had pangs of jealousy over Ariel's joy at having a daughter. Rachel loved and adored her two sons, but she so badly wanted a daughter. Unfortunately, these things cannot be preordained. The next best thing would be to bestow the most lavish dresses and girly clothes on her new niece.

Samantha was a beautiful child, and the four children got along as close as brothers and sisters. Heschel and Jacob both had great marriages and close ties to family. Boston was becoming a bustling city, and lots of new housing was cropping up. People were refurnishing and redecorating, and business was great.

With a growing family, the two brothers decided to move up and buy single-family houses near each other with good school systems in safe neighborhoods. Immigration was coming at such a fast pace, and the city streets were becoming crowded and overrun. They found two houses in a small suburb of Boston called Brookline. It was a quiet community with many Jewish immigrants and a good school system. It bordered on Boston, and the trolley car was nearby that could take them into the city anytime they wanted.

They each had a fenced-in backyard for the children to play and to entertain. Life certainly had its ups and downs, but right now, it felt perfect. One block away was a street laden with shops and groceries of every kind.

Was there any place on earth more perfect than this? Rachel thought.

Then the war happened. In December 1941, the Japanese bombed Pearl Harbor in Hawaii and drew America into the war.

Men were sent overseas, and women became the laborers. Steel mills were run by women who became riveters and mechanics.

Being a stay-at-home mom was no longer an option for Rachel and Ariel. They could not work full-time, but they devised a schedule where Rachel would watch Ben and Samantha while Ariel would go to work and Ariel would watch Steven and Benjamin when Rachel would go to work. Jacob hated to see her do this but felt she needed to help the war effort, and by now, his work was spiraling down again. So two days a week, the women left their children and put in their time at the boot factory. It was a mere trolley stop from home, and the days went by fast.

This way of life was certainly nothing anyone had anticipated, but at least they had each other. When it wasn't too cold outside, they would have backyard barbecues and the kids would play. How long could this war last, anyhow? Each day, they would listen to the radio announce how many American men had perished. This made them cling on to each other even more.

Jacob knew that he must have some relatives who had never gotten out of Poland. He did not know who they were, but Max and Sarah must have had relatives there. Hitler was on the move, and his warped sense of reality was becoming real to so many people. Jews were being persecuted here and abroad due to his rambling lies. So many were flooding the borders of the USA and Canada, and people didn't want them anymore. Americans were entitled, and most began as immigrants anyhow but quickly forgot their roots. This was never the case with Jacob, nor was it with Heschel.

Jacob thought about Jordanna a lot and wished he knew what had happened to her. It was another time and another place. It seemed as though it was a whole lifetime ago, but in actuality, it had only been a little more than twenty years.

Life developed a rhythm. There was always food on the table, a roof over their heads, and the love and support of a wonderful family, albeit this included neither Max nor Esther. Often, Jacob would think about David and would wonder what he would be doing now. Possibly drafted? He hoped not, but he could not bring himself to call to find out. There was a limit to how much toxicity he would expose himself to.

Business stayed on a steady line. The three men worked hard at whatever business they had, and they certainly had a following that sustained them. Over the years, Anthony had gotten married and was now expecting his first child.

Then it was September 1945.

Headlines screamed, "THE WAR IS OVER!"

Once again, Rachel and Ariel were both pregnant and due within weeks of each other. They both vowed that this would be the last time, no matter what. Ariel wished for a healthy baby, but secretly, both wished for a healthy little girl for Rachel.

Everyone was celebrating in the streets. Car horns were honking, and people were kissing and hugging strangers. In the aftermath of the war, the atrocities of the Nazis came to the surface, and all people could do was shake their heads and wonder, "How?"

As men returned from the war, the reality set in. Boston was a growing city, but the housing shortage created an immediate problem for the throngs of immigrants arriving daily. Both Rachel and Ariel lived just outside the city in a middle-class residential area. Houses began to go up at a rapid pace. Business was bustling.

Still, there was a steady black film that seemed to encompass the whole community. So many people walked around in a half-dazed world. They all had numbers tattooed on their arms. These were the actual survivors of Hitler's camps. No matter how much both Ariel and Rachel tried to approach these people with kindness and gifts, their hollow eyes would wander and not really understand the kindness. Brookline was loaded with immigrants coming over from Europe, and there did not seem to be much help.

With this in mind, Rachel approached one of the rabbis in the local shul. "Rabbi, there must be something we can do. These people are walking around half-dead."

The rabbi agreed. "But, Rachel, what can we do? These people have been so displaced."

"Let's have a weekly social where everyone can come together. This can be totally without any form of stress or expectation. Just a place to mingle and have some hot coffee and Danish. Maybe even meet others from their own community. It is possible that they can even meet others from their own community and find out what has become of others that they knew. These people have had no kindness or softness in their own lives for so many years. They have witnessed death and destruction."

So it was that on the following weeks posters went up along the streets and businesses promoting a social get-together to become acquainted with their new neighbors. Of course, refreshments would be served. The other announcement decried the fact of the possibility that missing relatives could be located. They just needed to show up.

The flyers were a hit. Hundreds of people showed up that night. It was overwhelming. Rachel and Jacob and Ariel and Heschel split up and took all the information they could. By the end of the evening, they were spent but also loaded with paperwork to help these people possibly find their loved ones.

This was not how this began. Rachel, growing larger by the minute with child, and Ariel, not far behind, could not believe they had undertaken this responsibility; but on the other hand, neither ever felt so fortunate to be where they were in their lives at this moment.

And so it was that Rachel and Ariel became the martyrs of Brookline. It became an undertaking so large that neither could ever have expected.

Once again, Rachel and Ariel were pregnant.

Chapter 52

November 26, 1946: She's Born

The excitement of November 26, 1946, was felt all over Brookline—no, maybe Boston. Rachel Kalinsky had a baby girl. They named her Sarah, after Jacob's mother. Rachel was a much-loved daughter of Boston by then, and the excitement of her having a girl, finally, permeated the air.

Rachel and Jacob were equally as excited. However, the baby did happen to arrive on Benjamin's birthday, and this was not exactly the birthday present he was expecting. So it was, after her first cry, Benjamin would sulk for days on end, not even acknowledging this baby who was now his sister. Oh well, so be it.

Life now seemed to be perfect. The years flew by. Ariel also had a baby girl named Bella, and this only cemented her relationship with Rachel even more. They now had three children each, all of the same ages, living feet apart, and would grow up as one happy family.

Life was so good in both Jacob's and Heschel's homes. There was a semblance of peace and tranquility that they had never felt before.

October 1947

Rachel had spent the last three months gearing up for Steven's bar mitzvah. The day was now upon us, and Jacob could not have been prouder of his son. Steven began studying for this day three years ago, and learning seemed to come easy for him. He was tall for his age, handsome, and very refined. He stood on the bimah in front of 150 friends and family members.

Jacob's heart swelled with pride. This was much different from his own bar mitzvah in Poland. Steven took the Torah from its home and marched it up and down the aisles of the temple. Everyone had an opportunity to touch the magnificent scroll with their prayer book or shawl. This was considered a privilege, and for Steven to carry the Torah, followed by his family and the rabbi, made him feel that he was indeed becoming a man that day. This was his rite of passage, and he performed it beautifully.

After he read from the Torah—in Hebrew, without skipping a beat—he faced his parents and thanked them for being the wonderful, supportive people they were. He came to tears as he told the congregation how much his parents had sacrificed to give him this day and how grateful he was. He even managed to thank his younger brother for putting up with him while he demanded quiet as he studied. With this, everyone laughed.

After the service was over, everyone went into the great hall of the temple, where tables and chairs were set up and a lavish lunch was served.

This was a milestone in Jacob's life. His only regret was losing all contact with his half-brother, David. He totally cut off all communication with Max and Esther, thereby cutting off all communication with David. He didn't know if David had gone to war or even if he was alive or dead.

Chapter 53

Boston 1948

Work was busy—almost *too* busy for the three men to handle. It was now 1948, and the postwar boom was affecting them all. Jacob and Company now had several people working for them, and money was no issue. Max and Esther had disappeared from Jacob's life, and other than thinking of David from time to time, he thought of no one. He had three happy and healthy children whom he loved, with a wonderful homelife and, of course, Rachel. His love. Then it all changed.

"Hello, my landsman. I understand you are the finest artisan in the city."

The voice was unmistakable. Jacob had never revealed his shame to anyone his entire life. Now this gravely and harsh voice was circling his senses.

As he turned around, he noticed the one discernable feature: There was a missing thumb. There could now be no mistake. His heart was thumping a hundred beats a minute, and his hand was shaking. He knew he had to compose himself.

As Jacob turned to look into the face of the man who had molested him almost thirty years ago, he forced himself to smile. "Yes, can I help you?"

"My name is Josef, and I come from Koretz, as I heard you are also from. I need some furniture refurbished, and your name kept coming up as being the best. Will you be able to come and look at the work I have and possibly restore it for me?"

Jacob had to think fast. He was, by now, certain that this was the evil man who had accosted him so long ago. He never prepared himself for this situation.

"Of course, I will be happy to come and look those pieces over and give you a price." Josef gives Jacob his address and phone number. "Let me know when you can come. I look forward to hearing from you."

As Josef closed the door, Jacob came up behind him and, with trembling hands, quickly locked the door and put up the CLOSED sign. He had no idea how he was going to exact his revenge, but he knew he had to. Perhaps it was time to have a meeting with Heschel and Anthony.

It was a Friday afternoon, and dusk was fast approaching. It was not unusual for Jacob to put the CLOSED sign out a little early. Many of the residents were already on their way home to bring in the Sabbath. Jacob took a deep breath and called Heschel and Anthony to come to the shop. This was so out of nature for Jacob that Heschel and Anthony ran over as fast as possible, concerned that something terrible had happened to Jacob.

Now Jacob was faced with not only revealing this long-kept secret from his brother but also not knowing what to do with the information. Jacob was not a hateful man by nature, but he needed to exact some kind of revenge on this horrible person. It was an unbelievable situation that this man, this awful, miserable man would someday show up in his shop. This was thousands of miles from home and so many years later.

Finally, Heschel and Anthony came in. Jacob poured them each a strong drink and sat them down.

Heschel was totally confused, and showed it. "Jacob, what has happened? Is Rachel all right? Are the kids all right?"

Jacob's hand gesture was enough to let them know that this had nothing to do with the family.

He related the story of what had happened at Jordanna's home and how certain he was that Josef was the one and the same person who had done this shameful thing to him. He had never lost the hatred that he felt for this man, and it also explained a lot of why he hated Max so much.

Heschel sat with his mouth wide open, unable to speak. Being so much younger and having been born in this country, Anthony did not know what to think.

"Say something, please, say something," Jacob begged. "I have kept this secret buried all these years, and a huge weight has been lifted from my shoulders now that I have shared my secret."

Heschel was the first to speak. "My brother, there was a time at Jordanna's when your nature seemed to change overnight. You became quiet and sullen and slept with the door to our bedroom barricaded. Now I understand why. I should have been able to be there for you."

"No, Heschel, it was my job to protect you. You were too young. The question now is, what to do?"

The information needed some time to sink in. After all, what was the chance that these two men would come together again? Jacob knew that he would not rest until he exerted some kind of revenge on this man.

"Let's sleep on this for now. We will have to be very clever and cunning to create a pain so bad on this man without compromising our own safety or reputation. Heschel, for now, please do not tell Ariel what I have shared with you. I am not prepared to share this with Rachel yet."

Anthony was at a loss for words. The knowledge of what had happened to Jacob tore at his heart. He had never heard a story like that before. Being born in this country and being younger, he was shielded from much of what had gone on overseas before and during the war.

Anthony was, however, brought up in the north end of Boston and was not a foreigner to crime stories. Living in the north end was like living with hundreds of family members. His own family was made up of hardworking people who led respectable lives, but they were never far from people who had no scruples. His family was highly regarded in his neighborhood. No one in his immediate family ever got in trouble and were well-known for their generosity.

Because of this, they could, if need be, call in favors from many of the less-than-respectable members of the community. With this thought, his mind began churning. There was nothing he wouldn't do for either Jacob or Heschel. He couldn't love them more if they were related by blood. He did understand, however, that this was an area he had to tread lightly on.

"Listen, Jacob, I know you will not rest until you can get some kind of revenge on this man. I also know that you do not have a mean bone in your body, but this man did something so outrageous to you, and I want you to achieve some sort of satisfaction for that. You have carried this load for so long. If God did not want you to find a way to release your misery over this, he would not have sent this man to your shop. I mean, what would the likelihood of that happening if it were not divine intervention?"

"I don't know how far you want to go with this, but know I will do everything in my power to help you achieve some semblance of peace with this. I suggest you begin by contacting this person and get to know him. He must not know who you are at this time though. We will take our time and think this through. You are not alone with this anymore."

The following day, Jacob called Josef and set up an appointment to see him at his home on Monday. He had no idea how he would react upon seeing him again. At least he knew what he was dealing with and prepared himself to act as cordial as he normally would.

As he approached Josef's home in the town of Waltham, a little northwest of Boston, he was unimpressed. It was a two-family duplex in a lower-middle-class section of Waltham. For some reason, he expected it to be in a better part of town.

Jacob rang the doorbell, and a portly middle-aged woman answered the door. Clearly, this was Josef's wife.

"My husband asked me to meet with you and give you an idea of what we are looking to do. He will be home shortly. Unfortunately, he was detained."

Her name was Stasha, and although she was not terribly attractive, she had a kind demeanor about her.

"May I offer you a beverage?" Her English was not so clear, but Jacob got the idea.

"No, thank you. I would like to see what you need done and be on my way. Do you have a specific time frame that you need the work completed?"

With this question, she merely shrugged and answered, "Josef will be home soon."

Stasha led Jacob into her dining room, which had eight upholstered side chairs. "We really need to have life put back into the wood on these chairs and also to find fabric to reupholster."

She then led him into the living room that clearly was a bit worn and tired. "Jacob, I find this room very sad. We want to make it a more joyful room. New fabrics, new upholstery, and, how you say, a buffing up. Can you help do this?"

Just then a key turned in the door, and Josef came rushing in. "So sorry to keep you waiting. I hope Stasha gave you some idea of what we are looking to do."

"Yes," replied Jacob. "You and Stasha can feel free to come into the shop and go through fabric swatches to pick out what you would like. From there, I can give you an estimate as to what the cost will be to get all the work done."

"Oh, wait, Jacob. The most important piece of all is in my office. I brought it over from Europe and want to restore it to its original luster."

With that, Josef escorted Jacob into his office off the long hallway and showed Jacob the piece he was so proud of.

Jacob could barely contain his shock. "Where, might I ask, did this beautiful piece come from?"

"Believe it or not, it was left behind at a woman's home in Koretz, Poland, after the war. When I saw it, I knew I wanted it for its beautiful lines and curved wood. It spoke to me."

The piece was the same divan that had caught Jacob's attention when he had first arrived at Jordanna's home. He could barely keep from shouting Jordanna's name. At the very least, he would find a way to ultimately know the destiny of Jordanna. He began to feel faint and knew he had to get out of there.

"When you choose your fabrics and I order them, then I will take your pieces to my shop, and we will begin working on them," Jacob said. "Until I know the cost of your fabrics, I cannot give you a solid price. I will, however, begin an estimate based on the labor to make these pieces like new again."

With that, he left, with hardly a breath left in his lungs. He thought for sure he was going to pass out. What was the possibility of any of this happening? First, Josef shows up and now the divan.

I must get to Heschel and let him know what is happening.

Jacob's hatred for this man was growing by the minute. How could he exact revenge on him without jeopardizing his own future and that of his family? The thought of even seeing Josef again horrified him. Thank God he had Heschel and Anthony to lean on with this information.

As soon as Jacob arrived at the shop, he told Heschel what had just evolved. Heschel was as shocked as Jacob was to hear about the divan.

"Now we know for certain that Josef is the evil monster that attacked you," Heschel said. "Let's sit down with Anthony and figure out a plan. It's not going to be easy. We have to get the job done as if he were any other customer and keep in his good graces. He must not find out who we really are and what the connection is until we're ready. This man must pay for what he has done."

Josef called the following day to let Jacob know that he and Stasha would be coming by on Wednesday to look at fabrics. As soon as Anthony found this out, he insisted on being there as well. Having him and Heschel there made Jacob feel much more relaxed.

Chapter 54

Josef

Josef was born into a military family at the end of the nineteenth century. He never quite knew his exact birthday but assumed it was around 1888. In 1912, he entered the Polish army and was eventually stationed near Koretz.

He loved being in the military. It gave him the kind of power and respect that the uniform afforded him. In Koretz, he had a lavish bedroom in a clean and upscale boardinghouse taken over by the Polish army. It was near the center of town, and his main job was to walk the streets and secure the nights.

One of the benefits of his job was his access to a lively brothel run by a highly respected madam. It was not unusual for him to drop some of his pay at least once a week there. It was a lively place, and the women were not like the women who frequented the streets.

At one point in early 1919, he noticed a young man coming and going in the house. Eventually, he quietly followed him up the stairs one night and saw him go into one of the bedrooms. After asking around, he was told that there were two young men staying at the home until their father sent for them.

Although Josef had a lust for women, he also had a proclivity for little boys. It was not something he was proud of, but his secret was his alone. In fact, he hardly gave in to it. The knowledge that he had a perfect prey just up the stairs made it too easy to overlook. There was always a lot of noise and music playing in the living room, and if he was careful, he could sneak away without notice.

So it was on this particular evening, he snuck upstairs and let himself into the bedroom shared by Jacob and Heschel. He surveyed the room, closed the door, and immediately cupped his hand over Jacob's mouth as he relieved him of his pajama drawers. With a menacing whisper, he let Jacob know that he was not to make a sound, nor was he to tell anyone, or his brother would be next.

After Josef finished taking his way with Jacob, he could hear the boy muffling sobs. He knew the boy would never be able to identify him, so he made himself presentable and quickly left the room.

As Josef made his way downstairs, he waited in the living room with everyone else, making sure the boy did not come down. In the living room of this brothel, there stood a beautiful carved divan that had always caught his eye. It was here that he would sit for the next ten nights eyeing the stairway. He felt secure that the boy would never say anything, and he never saw him again.

Josef was also aware of the rumblings of the Soviet army due to a territorial dispute dating back to the Polish-Russian Wars. It was also due to a difference of ideology. Josef had little time to decide whether to be a warrior and defend his homeland or to defect. Being the coward he obviously was, his decision was clear. He would book passage on a ship to America and leave before the uprising began.

This was not information he shared with anyone, but he did inform the owner of the brothel that things might get heated and she may want to leave her spot in this town before the Bolsheviks began arriving. She still had plenty of time, but he wanted her to have enough time to make arrangements.

Jordanna could not believe what she was hearing but took great stock in it. She thanked him for his kind warning and asked how she could repay him. Josef replied that he had become very fond of this beautiful divan and would be happy to buy it from her.

"My divan? This is what you want?" She could hardly believe she heard right.

Why, she asked herself, *would this young soldier want this piece of furniture?*

"If you want it, you shall have it. If I must think about making a hasty move from my home, it will be one less thing I have to think about."

So it came to be that after some time had passed, Josef loaded the divan onto the large ship headed for America and headed for the land of plenty. He had money in his pockets and his first piece of furniture.

Chapter 55

The Plot

On Wednesday, at precisely 1:00 p.m., Josef and Stasha came through the door. Heschel was the first to greet him. Josef could not tell that Heschel was sizing him up with much disdain. Jacob and Anthony came up behind Heschel, and Jacob made all the proper introductions.

In the back of the shop was a room filled with samples of fabrics. There was a long table in the center of the room where customers could lay the samples out as they perused them. It was there that Jacob led Josef and Stasha and got them situated.

"I must go back to work, but when you have made your decisions, come and get me. If you need anything in the meantime, we will be in the front of the shop."

As Jacob returned to the front of the shop, both Heschel and Anthony looked at Jacob stone-faced. They could now put a face to the name. It was only a week ago that they even knew anything about Josef.

Anthony was the first to speak. "Jacob, I will not let you down. I have come up with some ideas, but first, we must take this man's money and get his furniture taken care of. This is going to take careful planning, but I will have a way that we can seek our revenge without putting ourselves or our families in danger. We must be able to keep him in our sights so that we know his comings and goings."

Jacob and Heschel both agreed with Anthony. For the time being, they would be professional and work to get the job done.

Jacob never stopped thinking about his family and how much he loved them. He had his Rachel and his three children whom he absolutely adored. Of course, if truth be told, Sarah, his youngest, was his favorite. Partly because she was a demure little girl but also because she was named for his mother.

Rachel's parents had moved close to Boston, and every Friday night, they would come to Jacob and Rachel's home to welcome in the Sabbath. Rachel's parents were also a constant fixture during the week, and this gave Rachel a break from mothering. They were totally devoted to their grandchildren and loved Jacob like a son.

Rachel and Ariel continued to have their monthly socials that were a huge hit. By now, the immigrant population was so large that they had at least fifty or more volunteers to help carry the load. A small office was set up in Coolidge Corner, the heart of Brookline, and this was supported by various donations. It never ceased to amaze them how many families were brought together due to their efforts.

It also never ceased to amaze them how grateful people were to just find out what had happened to their families over in Eastern Europe. More often than not, the news was jarring. Sometimes they would find family members had fled to Argentina, and they would help track them down. The Kalinsky name held a lot of weight in the Boston area, and it was mostly due to Rachel's and Ariel's commitment.

Jacob was mulling all this around in his mind when he suddenly heard Josef calling him from the back room. He had been so deep in thought that he almost forgot Josef and Stasha were still there.

"Jacob, I think we have made our decisions."

Jacob could hardly believe that this smiling and seemingly kind man was the perpetrator of all nightmares.

Grabbing a pencil and notepad, Jacob began jotting down fabric names, colors, numbers, and pattern repeats, putting the names to a specific piece of furniture. The special divan called for a dark green velvet that made Jacob think of Greta all over again.

"Josef, I will put together an estimate based on all these fabric selections and get it right out to you. If you agree, I will require a deposit, and we will bring your pieces into the shop and get to work."

Josef and Stasha left the shop that day with more excitement than they had had for a long time. It was a new project and would transform their home. Little did they know that eventually their smiles would be turned upside down.

Jacob had to keep reminding himself who this man was. Jacob was such a kind soul that when he looked at Josef, he almost forgot the monster that lived within the man.

The following week, the estimate arrived at Josef's home, and the week after that, Jacob, Heschel, and Anthony arrived to bring his furniture to the shop. This gave Anthony an occasion to look over Josef's home in case he had to know where everything was for the immediate future. A plan was forming but had not yet taken shape. They still had time.

As the weeks passed, Josef would drop into the shop to see the progress taking place. Mostly, he was interested in the divan. This was like a knife cutting through Jacob's heart, but he never let it show.

"Jacob, this piece, more than all the rest is very special to me. I keep it in my office and am truly the only one that uses it. It reminds me of home and a special place I used to frequent. Bringing it over to this country was not easy, but I'm glad I made it work."

It seemed that every time Josef opened his mouth to speak, Jacob would be jolted back to Jordanna's. Soon the work would be finished, and Jacob would get paid in full. It was then that he would seek his revenge.

Anthony kept telling him to hold on for now. He had developed a plan, and the less that Jacob knew, the better. Anthony would never forget how Jacob brought him into the business and gave him a career. Jacob and Company had become a very busy and profitable company. The three men had comfortable lives with families, and Anthony would never allow anything to jeopardize that. He thought of Jacob and Heschel more as brothers than as partners.

At the time, the north end of Boston was known for great Italian food, festivals in the street, and close-knit families. It was also known for harboring criminals and loan sharking. Anthony and his family were as clean as snow but would often do favors for some of these so-called syndicates. There were always rumors around, but if one kept to themselves and kept their nose clean, one could consider themselves safe. Living in the north end of Boston was like being part of a large family. It didn't seem to matter which family one belonged to. It was always good to have someone beholden rather than the other way around.

To Anthony, asking someone to do something less than legal was not in his nature. He approached his father. With Jacob's permission, he told his father the whole story and asked for his help.

"Papa, I want to help Jacob get the resolution he needs so badly but cannot put him nor his family in any kind of danger. I want this Josef to know what it is like to suffer, and I want him to find out who Jacob is in the end but need you to guide me as to whom I should approach with this."

"Anthony, I have never asked anyone in this neighborhood for anything, but I always knew that if I needed a favor, I could go to anyone. When you were a little boy, I always sent you to the barbershop to help with errands. You would always complain, but I knew what I was doing. You were the kid that everyone could trust to get an errand done, sweep the shop, walk someone home. I never allowed our family to be beholden to anyone but racked up situations so that if I ever needed a favor, I could feel free to ask. I think the time has come to cash in on one of those favors now."

"Papa, I don't really want to physically hurt this man. I want to frighten the hell out of him, maybe run him out of town and let him know who he is dealing with. I think Jacob would be happy if this man were to leave Boston and never return. There is also a piece of furniture he has that must remain with Jacob. I think that will hurt him more than anything. I don't know what the attachment is to this certain piece, but I know it means a lot to Jacob, and apparently, it does to Josef as well."

"I will call Uncle Mario tomorrow and arrange a meeting with him. You don't have to involve Jacob. We'll take care of the matter and make certain of the outcome first. Jacob is like a son to me as well, and it hurts and angers me to think of what he has had to endure. I agree, this man must pay."

Once Jacob had the fabric at the shop, he, Anthony, and Heschel brought several pieces of Josef's furniture over to begin the work. The one piece that Jacob made sure to get last was the divan. He knew that no matter what, he was never going to let that piece go. His plan was to deliver everything else first and get paid with the promise that the divan would follow. He didn't even care if Josef held back some money to cover what he had not yet received. Once the furniture was delivered, Anthony would take care of getting satisfaction for Jacob.

During the following ten, weeks either Josef or Stasha had become a frequent visitor to see Jacob and watch the progress. To say they were thrilled with the work would be an understatement. Little did they know what was in store. Josef never could have guessed that Jacob harbored so much hatred for him.

Jacob never shared any of this with Rachel. He had his wonderful family, three children whom he worshiped and adored. A wonderful home in a great neighborhood filled with other couples like himself and Rachel. The children were happy and well-adjusted. If it weren't for Josef, his life would be perfect.

Every time he laid eyes on that man, his mind would be brought back to that awful night. No matter how friendly Josef pretended to be, Jacob could not, would not allow himself to soften. He had been filled with so much hatred for this man for so long.

He often had nagging thoughts about Jordanna and would wonder incessantly about what had happened to her. Did she get out of Poland before the war began? He would love to know how Josef ended up with the divan from Jordanna's home. Did she have to flee and leave everything behind? Had Josef taken liberties with other people in her home? He wished beyond hope that he could somehow find out what had become of her.

Finally, most of the furniture was complete. Jacob explained to Josef that the divan was being held up because the fabric was coming from abroad and he needed more time to complete it. Josef showed a bit of agitation over this, but there was nothing more that could be done. Jacob assured him that the minute the fabric arrived he would complete the piece and deliver it. He swore that when Josef eyed it, he would know it was worth waiting for.

Meanwhile, Josef had all the other pieces in his home and was ecstatic over the workmanship. Stasha, oddly enough, seemed to be secondary in the planning of this. Typically, it was the woman of the house who took care of furnishings and fabrics. Little by little, Josef was showing his true colors. The facade was being stripped. Only a controlling man would behave the way Josef did.

Jacob first witnessed it when Josef showed his short temper in front of him and Heschel. Stasha must have overstepped her boundaries with him, and Josef's clenched fist was noticeable. He was easily agitated and always had to be in charge, always had to have the last word. Jacob was feeling more and more secure in exacting revenge on this nasty man.

When Jacob presented Josef the final bill for the work done, he did not even ask to hold anything back for the divan. He told Jacob that he trusted him and that his workmanship was above reproach. He would pay in full at this time with the hope that the divan would be following in no more than two weeks' time. Jacob assured him that it would be complete by then.

Jacob quickly called Anthony and gave him a timeline.

Anthony's reply was succinct. "Jacob, forget everything and just trust that all is being taken care of. I have a feeling that after next week, you will never lay eyes on this man again. The less you know, the better, but you should know that this man will know who you are. He will not have time to show up at your shop again for he and his wife will be driven out of town and never to return. Be assured that neither will be physically harmed and nothing will ever be traced back to you. You have my word."

Jacob became flushed with relief and let out a sigh so long that it seemed he had not breathed this entire day. If truth be told, he felt as if he hadn't taken a breath since Josef first appeared in his shop. He didn't know what Anthony had planned, and it was better that way. He trusted Anthony with his life and knew that whatever happened, Anthony would never let any harm come to Jacob.

When Jacob arrived home that night, he sat at the dinner table and looked around at his family. How could the son of a poor chicken farmer end up with so many riches? He loved his family with so much passion. When this whole Josef situation was finally over, he pledged to spend more time with Rachel and the children. Perhaps a long vacation at the shore next summer. All he knew was that he wanted to envelop them all, love them, and keep them safe always.

The following day was uneventful. Jacob went to the shop along with Heschel. There was certainly more work to be done than either had imagined. The radio was spouting words and images from a telecaster that knew just how to draw them in. His name was Paul Harvey, and neither Jacob nor Heschel could get enough of his ranting and raving about postwar. He was always happy to interject pieces of how the Jews were being treated. Many were almost catatonic.

Anthony called Jacob early in the day and told him that he would not be at his shop for a couple of days.

"Not to worry, all is fine," he said.

Anthony also told Jacob that it would best to not have any contact with Josef during the following week. He said no more, but it really wasn't necessary. Jacob knew something was going down, and the less he knew, the better.

Jacob told Heschel what Anthony had related to him.

"My brother, you have carried this burden on your shoulders for so long. I am happy to be able to share some of this weight with you. In a short time, this torture will be over, and Josef will get his due."

No more words were uttered. It was not necessary. The men would go on about their business as if everything was normal and wait to hear from Anthony. They couldn't imagine what was going to happen.

Jacob came home that night with pockets full of candy for the children and flowers for Rachel.

"What in the world are we celebrating?" Rachel asked.

"Can't I bring my beautiful wife flowers without necessarily celebrating anything special? I know I have been a little distant recently, and this is my way of apologizing. Life is too good to be absorbed in anything other than my family and all the riches we have. Since the war has ended, I have seen so much suffering. So many people displaced and so many people with empty eyes. I am very proud of the work you and Ariel have done to bring some semblance of relief to others. Our business has prospered, our family is healthy and happy, and I love my wife. Isn't that reason enough to bring home flowers? Perhaps I don't do it often enough."

The following week passed with no word from Anthony. If anyone asked why his shop was closed, Jacob would tell them he was on a short trip. Anthony's wife was brought up in the north end and knew when not to question any of Anthony's comings and goings. This was not the first time that he would give her the excuse that he had to go on a business trip and would return in a week's time.

Finally, the following Friday, an excited Anthony came in to the shop. After putting the CLOSED sign on the door, he sat Jacob and Heschel down and told them the saga of Josef and Stasha.

Jacob could now relax because he would never see them again.

Chapter 56

Execution of a Plan

Last Sunday, Anthony knew that Josef and Stasha would be out of town for the day. He explained to Jacob that he had arranged for several men from his neighborhood to go to Josef's home and empty it of everything: every piece of furniture, every piece of clothing, everything.

When nosy neighbors asked if Josef and Stasha were moving, they were told that Josef was called away and would be moving across country. Josef and Stasha were very private people to begin with, so no one questioned this. After the home was cleaned out, two of the men stayed behind and waited for Josef to return.

When Josef's headlights came down the street, the men did not wait for Josef to get out of the car. They grabbed Josef and Stasha and threw them in the back seat. Shaking with fear, Stasha begged for the two men to let them go. Josef was just perplexed as one of their abductors drove away.

"Have no fear. We will not harm you, but you are leaving Boston and will never return if you know what's good for you. It is time, Josef, for you to pay for your past sins."

Josef, still perplexed, did not seem to understand what sins this man was referring to. "Please explain yourself. You must have the wrong person."

"Think back, Josef. In 1919, Poland. A young man sleeping soundly in his bed, feeling safe until his life was shattered forever by an unimaginable affront to his body. Think back because you ruined this young man's life—that is, until now.

"Fear not, Josef, for we are not out to harm you, but be rest assured that if you ever step foot in Boston again, that promise will not be kept. All your belongings have been moved to a small house on the Canadian border in Caribou. It is a township in Maine, where a small cabin outside of the town has been equipped with all your furnishings and enough food and supplies to last a week. After that, you are on your own. Periodically, some people will be expected to stay over while crossing the border. You will allow this if you know what is good for you. Also know that you will constantly be watched and checked on.

"There are pillows and blankets in the trunk, and we will soon stop and get them for you. Don't even think of getting out of the car. We will make a rest stop when we are sure we have come upon a desolate place where you can scream at the top of your lungs but no one will hear you."

Stasha had kept silent while listening to this, comprehending what was being said was not happening. So many questions unanswered. She was suddenly mute.

Anthony waited while Jacob took all this in. He was speechless.

"Anthony, what is to ensure that these two will not make it back to Boston and turn you and your friends in?"

"Jacob, unknown to Josef, the people living not more than twenty yards from them also work for the person whose cabin they are staying in. There will never be a time that the threat of leaving will be far from them. We will always know what they will be up to. We are not unreasonable people. The men who orchestrated this made sure that they would always have a supply of food, heat, and electricity. There is even a well on the property. They can live out their days in some form of comfort, but freedom to do as they wish is no longer an option."

"Anthony, what of Stasha? Did she understand why this is happening to them?"

"Jacob, what I came to find out was that years ago, Josef's nephew accused him of being less than appropriate with him. Of course, Stasha never believed this to be true, but the family never had anything to do with him again. It is not unimaginable to think that once a pervert, always a pervert. This new accusation made Stasha sit up and take notice. I am certain she is now becoming aware of what she is married to."

"Anthony, how can I ever repay you, your father, and your associates for taking care of this for me? I have spent my life trying to forget what this man did to me, trying to forgive my father for putting me in that position in the first place, but to no avail. I will always hate my father and blame him for every bit of unhappiness I have ever suffered in my life."

Anthony continued, "When he was brought into his new home, he was visibly shaken to see that all his furniture had been brought over and put in place. As soon as he realized that his precious divan was not there, he inquired about it. He was told that it was not only special to him but was special to that fifteen-year-old boy he had his way with all those years ago. It was as if a lightning bolt had hit him. He actually hung his head and nodded understanding."

Jacob almost felt sorry for the man. He had to keep reminding himself that Josef had apparently forced himself onto other children during his lifetime. Now it was time to bury this once and for all.

"Anthony, I will always consider you my brother. Please let everyone involved know that I am indebted to them for the rest of my life."

Dusk was approaching, and Jacob knew that Rachel would be getting ready for the Sabbath dinner. Her parents were coming over, and for the first time, Jacob could truly relax. He planned to keep this a secret from Rachel, but Heschel implored him to tell her. After all, she was his wife and would never think less of him. She was a strong woman, and this was a secret that should be shared. Jacob told Heschel he would think about it, wished him Good Shabbos, and headed for home.

Jacob first stopped by the corner grocery store near his house, picked up a bouquet of flowers for Rachel, and stuffed his pockets with candy for the children. It had become a custom for the kids to run up to him when he entered the house on Friday nights and rummage through his pockets for the bits of chocolates and nuts. Tonight was exceptional. His pockets were stuffed.

He ran up the steps of his home with a lighter gait than he had before. As expected, the children almost bowled him over as he came through the door. It was the weekend, and weekends were for family. It was wonderful to hear the laughter and screeching coming from these wonderful kids. His goal was to always provide a life for his family totally different than what he had experienced. He knew that as of now he had succeeded.

The kitchen was warm with wonderful scents of fresh bread and soup. Brisket was in the oven, and Rachel's mother was setting the table. Rachel's father was seated in the living room, reading the daily paper. It was a picture of serenity and love.

I am a lucky man, he thought to himself.

"Jacob, quickly wash up so we can light the Shabbos candles and sit down for dinner," Rachel said.

Jacob replied, "First, pick your head up and greet me properly."

He said this with a smile, and Rachel responded in kind. As soon as she saw the flowers, her smile turned into a huge grin and she threw her arms around Jacob and gave him a huge hug as the children giggled in the background.

This is the way Shabbos is supposed to be, he thought.

By the time dinner was over and the dishes clean, he was exhausted.

"Please, can we just stay up one more hour?" The children never wanted to go to bed, but Jacob needed some downtime this particular evening even more than usual.

Rachel's parents kissed everyone good night and headed for the door. They were wonderful to him and Rachel and the children. Tomorrow morning, he would go to services with Rachel, family in tow, and spend the afternoon at the zoo. There was a wonderful zoo in Boston, and the kids had been begging to go there. If truth be told, Jacob wanted to see the elephants even more than the children did.

The visit to the zoo turned out to be one of the most memorable days he had in years. The children screamed with glee at the sight of the gorillas and monkeys. The giraffes came right up to the fence and lowered their towering necks to say hi. Sarah's screams of delight were like music to Jacob's ears. He loved his children with a love he knew his own father never exhibited. More than likely never felt, however, for a brief time, he had an unconditional love from his mother. At times, he would feel her presence, and a knowing smile would come across his face.

At the end of the day, they had exhausted every animal and bird in the zoo and had eaten a huge share of candy, ice cream, and popcorn. *Where did the children put this?* he asked himself.

The ride home was quiet while all the children slept in the back seat of the car. As they approached their home, Jacob noticed that a strange car was parked in the driveway.

As they pulled up to their home, a very tall, handsome young man stepped out. He was somewhat familiar but was leaning on crutches. It was then that Jacob noticed that this young man was missing a leg.

"Hello, Jacob. It's been a very long time. I'm your brother, David."

Chapter 57

David

As soon as Jacob got over the shock of seeing David after so many years, he quickly threw his arms around him as tears ran down his cheeks.

"David, it's been so many years! What has happened to you?"

To this, Rachel chimed in, "For God's sake, Jacob, bring the man inside."

"Of course, of course. Please, David, let me help you in the house. I have so many questions."

Rachel ushered the sleepy children from the car and instructed them to get washed and ready for dinner. Jacob ushered David into the living room and offered him a drink. As Jacob poured a tall glass of scotch for his long-lost brother, the questions poured out of him.

"David, how did you lose your leg? Are Max and Esther still around? Have they changed at all?"

"Slow down. Let's take it one question at a time. Max became even more bitter when you and Heschel abandoned him. I'm sorry, *abandoned* is a bad choice of words. When you and Heschel decided to stay away, Max became a true version of what you always saw in him. He became sullen and nasty. He was never a warm, caring father in the first place, but life at home became intolerable."

"When Germany invaded Poland in 1939, he became nasty both to me and to Esther. In turn, Esther became a shadow of the mother she had been. She became as controlling to me as Max had been. As soon as I turned eighteen years old, I left home and joined the Marines. This fared well with neither Max nor Esther."

"Your name came up a lot at that time. He accused me of being no better than you, and truthfully, Jacob, I have always loved you and admired your strength. I had no choice at that time but to leave, or I would have died, anyway. My friends were enlisting, so I decided to join them. This was not a difficult decision, given the climate at home.

"When the Japanese bombed Pearl Harbor in 1941, I was stationed in Hawaii but was on a forty-eight-hour furlough when Pearl Harbor was attacked. I actually had flown over to the mainland when the attack occurred but quickly was sent back to Hawaii. It was a chaotic mess. So many of my friends died that day. As bad as things were, my main objective was to fight Hitler. While most of my service was spent going from island to island in the Pacific, moving closer to Japan, some of us were offered the opportunity to enter the war against the Germans in the European Theater. It was during the summer of 1944 that I was sent over to the south of France, which was being occupied by German forces. It was there that a land mine went off close to me, and that's how I lost my leg. My biggest regret is not getting to kill a Nazi."

"I was sent back to a military hospital in the States, where I got lots of rehab. After a while, I went home to visit Max and Esther. They had aged considerably. Neither was in great health, but I found that I couldn't even feel sorry for them. I stayed and helped out for a short while until one morning, Max did not wake up. He died a lonely, sullen, nasty man. I got to understand why you and Heschel left him. I may have lost my leg, but being in the service taught me what it was like to have a real family. Esther may be my mother, but she was never motherly. I couldn't take her controlling nature any longer."

"I helped her sell the farm and move into a retirement community. She'll still be lonely and miserable, but I do not feel any responsibility to her. I've done some travelling around, mostly visiting families of my brothers in war, but was hoping there would be some room in your heart to welcome me back into your fold and get to know my real family."

"David, your story is amazing. I had no idea where you were or what had happened. I guess I always assumed you were still living with Max and Esther, helping out at the farm. I really want you to get to know your nieces and nephews. I, of course, have one girl and two boys, but Heschel has two girls and one boy. I can have them over in a moment's notice. Heschel will be overjoyed to see you."

It was no more than a half an hour later that the front door burst open and a jubilant Heschel came through the door trailed by his three children and lastly, Ariel. The excitement was palpable.

"David, my long-lost brother, how are you?"

It was then that Heschel noticed a leg missing and, as tears ran down his cheek, asked the question: "David, what on earth has happened to you?"

It was then that David told the whole story over again.

"David, I had no idea that any of this had taken place. Neither of us even knew of Max's passing. Let's hope that we can put all of this behind us and become the family that we always wanted."

A boisterous voice rang out from the kitchen. "Come, sit down and eat. I've made enough for an army."

The happy chatter around the dinner table suddenly invigorated the children. They were always happy when with their cousins, but this was an especially important evening. They had all heard bits and pieces of conversation about their uncle David but never really put the story into perspective. Now he was here, and it was like a new family was formed.

Jacob was the first to speak up. "David, do you have a place to stay?"

David replied, "Yes, I have a room in a large brownstone in the south end of Boston. I didn't want to assume that Boston would be my permanent residence until I saw how I was welcomed by all of you. You have no idea how heartwarming your response has been."

"David, you may not be aware of this, but Heschel, me, and one other person, who is like a brother to us, are running a rather large upholstery and refinishing business. We have two shops, and we can certainly find a place for you. Given your leg situation, we can train you as a stitcher so you won't be on your feet all day. What do you say? Will you give it a try?"

This was more than David had ever hoped for. Between the warm welcoming and now a job opportunity, his heart was bursting with happiness.

"Jacob, I don't even need to think this over. Having the opportunity to work with both my brothers is more than I ever could imagine. Max will be rolling over in his grave."

"It's settled then. Take as much time as you need, and then we'll get you started."

The following Monday, David reported to the upholstery shop. Jacob made certain that Anthony came over and introduced him to his brother. He knew that in no time David would come to love Anthony and consider him family as well.

The following weeks proved to be a successful collaboration. David was a quick learner and often had been made to leave the shop for the evening or he would have stayed there all night. Ariel and Rachel began drumming up prospective dates for him as well. The social clubs they had formed years ago had blossomed in size, and there was no shortage of single women there. David was tall, handsome, and kind. How these three boys had turned out to have such big hearts was an enigma. They certainly learned from Max how not to be.

Soon, another Labor Day came around. It was the first Monday of September 1950. The Kalinsky family had one of the first television sets in the neighborhood. Every Friday night, after Shabbos dinner, the entire family would sit around the TV and take delight in watching the shows. The family saga of *I Remember Mama* was a favorite, and now that David was in their lives, he never missed an opportunity to join them for the Friday-night festivities. Rachel's parents were overjoyed when they heard about David. It was as if they had another son. Yes, life was perfect.

At this time, Benjamin was also preparing for his bar mitzvah, which was still a year away. As the business grew, it seemed that the size of this event grew along with it. Money wasn't a problem, so

Rachel made sure that Ben's bar mitzvah would be the event of the season. Steven was in his last year of high school, had his driver's license, and seemed to be fending off young women as if they were flies. Sarah was, by all accounts, the bratty little sister who loved tormenting her brothers.

The family could have been a Norman Rockwell painting. The happiness and contentment spilled over. Often, Jacob would pinch himself to make certain he was not living in a dream.

Chapter 58

End of an Era

David had become such an integral part of both the business and the Kalinsky family that it was difficult to remember a time he was not there. He had received a recent phone call that Esther was in the hospital and was failing. At this point, he felt compelled to visit her.

As he approached her hospital room, he hardly recognized the shriveled-up woman in the bed. She was hooked to oxygen, and her eyes were closed.

"Mother, it's David. I came as soon as I heard."

With that, she opened her eyes and stared intently at David. "You are not David. My David is off fighting a war in Germany, defending our country. You are too old to be David."

It was then that David realized she suffered from dementia and his visit would be futile. Esther closed her eyes again and drifted off to sleep.

The nurse informed David that his mother was sleeping most of the time and would probably not even remember that he was there. It would be just a matter of time before Esther would be gone for good. David had no remorse for the past years when he had no contact at all, but seeing that small, wrinkled woman lying in that bed did offer him some compassion. He was, after all, not a monster.

Three weeks later, David got the call from the hospital that Esther had passed. He took it upon himself to contact a local funeral home and make all the preparations for her service and burial. There was an empty plot next to where Max was buried, saved for this occasion.

David was shocked to learn that both Heschel and Jacob were planning to come to her funeral. They explained to David that they were not going out of respect for her—they had none—but out of love and support for David.

It was a small funeral. Other than the Kalinsky boys and their spouses and children, only a handful of people attended. It was a testament to the person Esther was. She never invited anyone in; therefore, there was no one to mourn. She was buried next to Max, and with a final goodbye, David knew that he would probably never visit this site again.

The following year went by so fast. Benjamin's bar mitzvah was fast approaching, and David had met a wonderful woman through a social club at the temple. Both Rachel and Ariel could not have been happier. He was planning to bring her to Ben's bar mitzvah and make their relationship solid. Since coming to Boston, his relationship with his brothers and their families was so natural that it was if it had never been different. He worked hard at the business, and every customer who came into the shop loved him.

Jacob, Heschel, and even Anthony loved having him around. His energy was infectious. The boys never told him about Josef and saw no reason to bring it up. Josef was out of their lives, and any thought of him was fleeting. Discussion of him would be like picking at a scab. It was finally over.

Ben's bar mitzvah studies were going well, and Rachel was tripping over herself to make certain that his event would be the envy of every boy in his bar mitzvah class.

The day finally arrived, and other than the fact that he had to share his birthday with Sarah, Ben had never been happier. Jacob's heart swelled with pride as he saw his son read from the Torah. This time, his uncle David was also there to receive an honor. It was called an aliyah, and everyone who received an aliyah would march up to the bimah and read a certain passage. This honor was presented only to people who were special to the boy being a bar mitzvah and his family. It was a glorious day.

Rachel wanted music and dancing, so the party following the service was not being held at the shul. She reserved a function room at a local restaurant, had it decorated to the nines, and hired a band to play games with the children and dance music for the adults. Once again, the event went off without a scar.

Through his happiness, Jacob was brought back to his own bar mitzvah in Poland. It may not have been a huge celebration, but he was elated as he marched down the street to the temple followed by friends and customers from the brothel. The outpouring of people was astonishing. Everyone celebrated his becoming a man. He would always cherish Jordanna for giving him that day.

David's girlfriend's name was Devorah. She could not have been lovelier. Devorah was born in Boston, and although she was Jewish, she was not really a practicing Jew. She and David fed off each other with a calming naturalness.

It was no surprise to anyone when David proposed shortly after Ben's bar mitzvah. Happy occasions were referred to as simchas, and there seemed to be no shortage of them. The wedding was planned for the following May. Steven was applying to colleges, making Jacob burst with pride. He would be the first Kalinsky to attend further education. Life could not be better.

New Year's Eve rolled around, and everyone sat around the TV to watch the ball drop in Times Square. The countdown began, and as the ball hit the ground, the children screamed with delight.

"Happy New Year!" they shouted.

The past year had been one of the best in Jacob's life, with the promise of an even better year to come. The year 1952 rolled in with much fanfare. Business was booming, the kids were healthy and happy and life was good. David fit in to the family as if he had always been there.

It was 1952, and Dwight Eisenhower was elected president. President Eisenhower had spent the previous forty years in the army, yet he exemplified home, hearth, and heaven. Even the Democratic candidate Adlai Stevenson liked him. Still, WWII was fresh in everyone's minds, and as new homes were being built, bomb shelters became a selling point.

David found himself yearning to return to the service but had to accept his fate. Yet he loved working alongside his brothers, and now that he had met Devorah, he was satisfied.

The winter months were spent with so many celebrations. David and Devorah had several engagement parties, and then Rachel and Ariel threw a lavish bridal shower for Devorah.

David bought a single-family home not far from Jacob and Heschel. The wedding day was drawing close.

It had never occurred to Jacob that a wedding announcement in the newspapers would attract all kinds of attention. It never occurred to Jacob nor to Heschel or Anthony that anyone in the East Coast would be able to see these announcements. Of course, neither David, Rachel, nor Ariel would have to think about this.

It had been years since Josef had been in their lives. Years since he had tarnished their thoughts. Why would they even think they had to concern themselves with this now?

A very long time had passed since they had a report on Josef. He was living a quiet life in Caribou, Maine. As far as they knew, Stasha and Josef were still in exile. Josef had years to build up resentment for being exiled to this godforsaken place. He, like so many others before him, felt that he was the victim. He never felt remorse or guilt for all the lives he had ruined.

The wedding day was finally here. Devorah made a beautiful bride. David was glowing with pride. Both Jacob and Heschel were his best men and Anthony an usher. Rachel and Ariel were picture-perfect in their rose-colored gowns with beaded accents. Sarah, being the youngest, was junior bridesmaid while the other children acted as attendants. The event was lavish.

As David brought his good leg down on the glass, "Mazel tov!" rang out in the congregation. Everyone was clapping and singing as the new Mr. and Mrs. Kalinsky strode down the aisle. When they got to the end of the aisle, they were instructed to create a receiving line. The brothers, along with Devorah's parents, lined up to greet their guests. One by one, the people strode by, kissing cheeks, offering warm wishes. It was one of the happiest events anyone had ever been to.

Suddenly, a familiar voice came up behind Jacob.

"Hello, Jacob." The voice was unmistakable. "It has been two and a half years since you sent me into exile. It may not be today and it may not be tomorrow, but when you least expect it, I will be waiting for you. No matter what you may think I have done to you, and I will never admit to it, you have managed to wreck my marriage and wreck my life."

With that, Josef slid out a side door as Jacob held on to a nearby railing. Never in his wildest dreams had he ever thought of anything like this happening.

David knew nothing of Josef, and Jacob wanted nothing to ruin this happy occasion. He decided to keep this information to himself until David and Devorah were off on their honeymoon.

The celebration that night was everything that David and Devorah had hoped for. Rachel and Ariel were off in such a gleeful mode that Jacob wanted nothing to do with ruining this night for them.

Oh, God, why? Haven't we all suffered enough? I have always shown so much gratitude for all my spiritual wealth and happiness. How could you throw this at me now?

At the end of the evening, Devorah changed into the most beautiful going-away outfit, with hat and gloves. She was a beautiful picture of what a happy bride should be. Their car was decorated with lots of silliness and streamers of cans and balloons. This was the epitome of happiness.

Their honeymoon was going to be at the Neville in the Catskills. This would be a new experience for both of them, but they really did not care if their honeymoon was spent in their car. They were in love. They were so meant for each other.

How could this dreadful person show up at this time in my life? Was I the chosen one to endure a lifetime of fear?

Josef's presence did not go unnoticed by David. After the receiving line ended, David approached Jacob and asked who this person was. He definitely did not get a good vibe from him.

"David, he was someone I knew from the old country and just wanted to stop by and say mazel tov. It's all good." There was no way Jacob would cast anything negative on this wonderful day.

The rest of the evening went by without a hitch. The black cloud that Jacob had over his head for most of his life was now back. David and Devorah would be off on their honeymoon, but Jacob would wait until tomorrow to let Heschel and Anthony in on what had just happened.

How, he asked himself, *did Josef leave Maine without being noticed?*

The following day, Jacob sat down with Heschel and Anthony and related what had happened at the wedding. They both were shocked.

Anthony was the first to speak. "Jacob, the first thing I will do is check to find out how Josef got away unnoticed. I will see my father and he will call his contacts and we'll get to the bottom of this. In the meantime, be aware. Always look at your surroundings, and be prepared for anything. I don't want to frighten you, but this man is dangerous. Just know that we all have your back."

The black cloud that seemed to have disappeared from over Jacob had returned. More than for himself, he was concerned for his family. Josef could be ruthless.

On Monday morning, Jacob and Heschel were in their shop, and Anthony was in his shop in the north end of Boston. By now, they all had several employees in each location, and Jacob felt safe in numbers. Besides the people working in the shops, there were always customers coming and going, and it seemed that half the police force would stop by on occasion for a cup of hot coffee that Jacob always had brewing.

There were many times that Jacob wanted to bring the police in and tell them what had gone on with Josef but was too afraid of implicating someone. No, he decided, he would wait it out and see what Josef had in mind. The one thing Jacob did do, however, was buy a gun and keep it as protection in a secure place. His intention was to never use it as anything other than a scare tactic should the situation present itself.

The first week passed without incident. Anthony's father found out that the people watching over Josef had taken some time away. It had been so long since Josef had moved into that house that they relaxed their guard. Little did they know that Josef was just lying in wait for the perfect opportunity to take off. No one had seen Stasha for many months, and since she was not their primary concern, they assumed that she had left him long ago.

On occasion, their home would be shared with a criminal element crossing the border from Canada. They knew that they were smuggling something over the border but never inquired. It wouldn't have done much good anyhow. These people traveled in pairs and usually only stayed a night. It would have been easy for Stasha to bribe them to take her away from this godforsaken place.

The property was gated, with guard dogs at the entrance. It would have been unlikely for Josef to get away unnoticed. Anthony's father promised to get to the bottom of things immediately.

David and Devorah returned from their honeymoon like two lovebirds. Ariel and Rachel could not wait to get Devorah in their clutches to hear about the honeymoon.

As soon as David walked into the shop, he noticed the suspicious glances between Jacob and Heschel.

"Okay, what is going on? I have been gone a little over a week, but it is obvious there is something I need to know."

At noon, a sign was put on the locked door of the shop that they were closed for lunch break. The shop cleared out, and Anthony arrived. The three men sat David down and told him everything. The astonished look on his face spoke volumes. He now understood more than ever Jacob's hatred for their father.

When all was explained, David was the first to speak. "Jacob, this man can be very dangerous. We must all look out for you, Rachel, and the children. Please let me know what I can do to help."

"David, first and foremost, you must not tell Devorah. Neither Rachel nor Ariel know of this, and we don't want to burden them with this now. When Anthony's father gets back to us with the report on Caribou, we will have a better idea of what we are facing."

Chapter 59

✦

Caribou

Shortly after Josef and Stasha settled into Caribou, things turned ugly. Stasha couldn't contain her anger. Months went by, and the hostility in their home became unbearable. Every now and then, a couple would appear for the night. They never knew nor did they ever question who these people were and where they were coming from or travelling to.

The neighbors several hundred yards down the road were constantly watching and checking on Josef and Stasha. They did, however, keep them stocked with plenty of food and water. The understanding directed to Josef and Stasha was that they never put up a fuss or question anyone who came to their door. The threat, apparently, was strong enough that Josef complied. He knew that he was at the mercy of someone, just not exactly who or where they were. There was a guardhouse at the entrance to the property, and two men were always on duty there with their guard dogs. It was likely that the residents and police of Caribou had an understanding that this property was off guard and anyone caught trespassing would be shot first, questions asked later.

Josef stayed aware of every timetable that was exercised by these people. He knew when the guards changed shifts and when the people next door would come or go. He also was aware of any route or trail that led away from the house that did not go by the entrance. He had all the time in the world to hatch an escape plan that he knew in time he would be able to execute.

The people coming over the border from Canada seemed to appear every four weeks, never any sooner. It was after one of these visits that Stasha's admonishment of Josef hit an all-time fever pitch, and without him even thinking, Josef's hands found their way around Stasha's throat. After she took her last breath, Josef knew what he must do. His hatred of her had built up so much over the past year that he felt no remorse over killing her. If asked where she was, he would just say that he woke up one morning and found her gone. How? He could not explain, just that she left.

In actuality, there could be many excuses for this. Their eyes were always on Jacob, so it could have been easy for her to hide in one of their visitor's cars or possibly to have bribed one of these people to take her away. After all, she was not their main concern. She had actually been gone for over a month before anyone even inquired about her. She had never been their primary concern, and if she found a way out, good luck to her.

Josef had no qualms about taking her out to the far side of the house one night and cut her body into pieces. He wrapped each piece into sheets and carried each one systematically into the woods so he could bury them in shallow graves. He would do this over a period of time to keep from attracting attention. It was always in the middle of the night, when everyone around him would be asleep. The dogs were always by the gatehouse at the entrance of the property, which was at least one-fourth of a mile away. He always went in the opposite direction and in the thickest of brush. No one ever caught on.

Two and a half years had passed from when he first arrived that he found his way out. He didn't have a car, so when the guard was relaxed one week, he walked to the highway and hitched rides back to Boston. Upon reading a local newspaper, he came across the upcoming nuptial announcement of a Kalinsky. He never knew about David, but because Rachel and Ariel had become such an integral part of the Jewish establishment in Boston and Brookline, the Kalinsky name always provided an alert to the media.

So it was that Josef hatched his little plan to find Jacob. The people in Caribou had not even had time yet to realize that Josef was gone. Everything happened so fast.

Chapter 60

Where's Jacob?

The week after David returned from his honeymoon, there had still been no sighting of Josef. The tension that Jacob was experiencing had to be hidden from Rachel and was increasingly becoming more difficult.

Finally, Anthony and his father arrived at Jacob's shop with the most discerning news. They sat Jacob and Heschel down and filled them in on what had been found when their associates went up to Caribou.

The cabin that Josef and Stasha had lived in showed no sign of life. It had only been ten days since Josef had been seen, but there was no sign of Stasha anywhere. None of her belongings were to be found. Upon searching the property, they came upon the shallow graves that Josef had dug. In one of them was Stasha's purse and identification, along with her body parts. Police could not be brought into this, so they constructed a bonfire and burned everything. Now they knew that a very dangerous man was on the run, and Jacob would most certainly be his target.

Several weeks went by without incident. Jacob had never been so nervous in his entire life. Anthony's friends very quietly took shifts watching Jacob's back and guarding his house. No one could let their guard down. Not now. Everyone felt responsible for allowing Josef to get away to begin with, and they would not rest until he was caught. What they would do with him after that was anyone's guess, but they knew they had to get rid of him once and for all.

During all this time, Rachel had no idea of what was going on around her. She noticed an unrest in Jacob but attributed it to his heavy workload. Her job was just to be supportive and not add any undue stress into Jacob's life.

With that thought, she never delved too much into his quiet moods. He did, however, seem to be more protective of the children, where they were going and with whom. He never wanted to see them go anywhere alone, and this she found worrisome. Eventually she would have to question him further as to why this sudden shift in their lives, but for now, she kept her thoughts to herself. How she loved him.

Six weeks passed since David's wedding, and there was a knocking on their door. Dinner had just gotten over, and the children were upstairs doing their homework. Rachel was in the kitchen cleaning up, and Jacob was watching the nightly news on TV.

Jacob jumped up with a start and ran for the door. He didn't have time to think or to prepare for who could be there. He opened the door to see the familiar back of a man hunched over. As he turned around to face Jacob, his worst fears were realized.

"Josef, what are you doing here?"

"Well, you ignorant immigrant who has ruined my life, I have come for payback. You could not possibly have thought that I would just let things go and disappear for good. If you value your family, you will not make a fuss but leave with me quietly."

Jacob's heart was pounding a mile a minute, but his concern for his wife and family made him comply. He noticed a bulge coming out of Josef's pocket, the pocket that housed his good hand. It would not have taken much for him to pull a trigger and get inside to possibly harm his family.

"Rachel," he called to his wife. "I have a customer that I have to bring to the shop to look at fabrics. I won't be long. I promise."

With that being said, Jacob grabbed his coat and hat and left the house with Josef. As soon as they drove off in Jacob's car, the men who had been watching the house came to the door to ask Rachel where Jacob was heading and with whom he was with. Josef had deliberately disguised his appearance when he came to the door, and Anthony's associates had no idea that it was Josef.

Rachel assured them that it was just a customer whom Jacob was taking to his shop.

To be on the safe side, they decided to follow up and go by the shop to make certain that Jacob was all right. As they approached the shop, they realized that there were no lights on.

"Where," they asked themselves, "could Jacob have gone?"

Several hours passed, and still no sign of Jacob. By now, everyone was concerned. Rachel called Heschel, who contacted Anthony and David. Everyone ran to be with Rachel and the children. Rachel had to finally learn what the possibility of Jacob's fate could be and why. She also had to learn that the police could not be brought into this.

It was time for Rachel to learn the truth. It was time for her to learn the deep, dark secret Jacob had kept for so long. The trouble was that the information was not coming from Jacob himself.

Heschel was the first one to speak. "Rachel, I have much to tell you that will explain Jacob's whereabouts right now. It relates to a secret that Jacob has carried with him his whole life. It was not until recently that he even shared his story with me and Anthony. For good reason, David has also just been let in on this. Before I go on, you need to understand that Jacob kept this secret only to protect his loved ones and also because he was so ashamed, even though he has never done anything to be ashamed of."

It was at this point that Ariel entered the home. The men, along with Rachel, were sitting behind the closed door of Jacob's study. As Ariel opened the door, she noticed a couple of men whom she had never seen before.

"Ariel," Rachel called out. "Please pour us all a drink and come sit beside me. I have a very bad feeling of what I am about to learn. Please sit."

With drink in hand, Rachel steadied herself for a truth long coming.

After a totally drained Heschel finished his story, Rachel could only remember to breathe. It was all too much to soak in. It was becoming all too much to endure.

"But, Heschel, where is Jacob now?" Rachel asked.

"We don't know. All we are certain of is that Josef has kidnapped him and taken him to God knows where. I'm sure you understand why the police cannot be called. We have come to learn that Josef has been making trips to the western part of the state recently. We are contacting all of Anthony's friends and relatives as well as business associates to be on the lookout for Jacob's car."

The sound that came out of Rachel's throat was guttural. As strong as a woman she has always been, this was too much to comprehend. First, she had to wrap her head around the fact that Jacob had been burying a dark secret from her all these years. Nothing would have changed the way she felt about him. If only he had trusted her enough to confide everything.

She loved him so much and was now faced with the prospect of never seeing him again. What could this horrible monster do to her Jacob? Where could he have taken him? Perhaps he was already dead?

Chapter 61

Stockbridge

When Jacob got into his car with Josef, he had no idea where he would be going or what was going to happen. He had to concentrate on the orders that Josef was giving him, which were directions to drive west. With a gun sticking in his ribs, Jacob was too afraid to make any sudden moves.

The one thing Jacob concentrated on was the road in front of him, beside him, and any signage they might pass. He had no idea where he was going or what was going to happen to him, but if he ever found himself out of this situation, he had to know how to get back or at least to get word to someone of his whereabouts.

"So, my great artisan, you have always known who I was and planned and plotted from the very beginning. How cunning of you."

To this, Jacob did not respond. His only defense at this time was to remain silent. His main concern was Rachel and the children. What would they be thinking? Would Heschel and Anthony tell Rachel about his past? His mind was racing a mile a minute, but he had to keep reminding himself to watch the road and be aware of everything around him.

Two and a half very long hours passed, and the road became narrower and narrower. There were no cars or people around anywhere. It seemed as though they were entering a dark void. It was very late at night, but the adrenaline surging through Jacob's body kept him awake and aware.

As they turned down a very narrow and windy dirt road, a house appeared at the end.

"I guess we're home for now, Jacob. This scene is very familiar to the exile you sent me to way up in Maine. This may not be Maine, but I'm sure there is no one around. You can scream your head off and ask for help, but no one will hear. You are about to get a taste of your own medicine."

To torment him further, Josef brought up Jacob's family. "You need not worry about your wife or children. I intend to handle you first and them after."

Jacob almost retched at the thought of this monster going anywhere near his family. Whatever it would take, he would have to find a way out. He had no idea of where he was. It was dark outside and difficult to read all road signs. He knew he was in the mountains, and from the direction he drove, he assumed that he was in the Berkshires. He knew he had to stay alert at all cost.

Josef instructed Jacob to pull over in front of the small house and to move slowly out of the car. The gun was never far from Jacob's torso. Josef led Jacob into the house. It was apparent that Josef had been planning this for some time. There was some furniture and boxes of provisions laid out on the kitchen counter.

"Josef, I have to use the bathroom—that is, if you have one."

"I am more sophisticated than you give me credit for, Jacob. Of course, there is a bathroom, but you are not to go alone."

In the dim light of the room, Jacob could see the black eyes of the devil in Josef's face. He was delighted with himself for pulling this off.

As Josef led Jacob out of the bathroom, he pulled a cloth out of his pocket and drenched it with a liquid from a can that sat nearby. He quickly held the wet cloth over Jacob's face until Jacob became a mound on the floor.

Now, Josef thought to himself, *I have you where I want you.*

Jacob would be out just long enough for Josef to get him positioned as he wanted him. When Jacob woke up, he would have no idea of where he was or what was about to happen to him. Josef was always a mean-spirited man, and this never changed but got more intense as the years went by. He took such delight in his plot for revenge on Jacob.

Strange how life turns out. The hunted became the hunter.

Chapter 62

A Secret Unfolded

When the children came downstairs to say good night, they were surprised to find their aunt, uncles, and Anthony in the house. It was important that Rachel keep her composure and not let on what had occurred just hours before. They had all constructed a story about Jacob's whereabouts. It was a work-related story that pulled Jacob away for a couple of days to look at a large job site.

They told the kids that Jacob hastily threw some things in the car and took off, not wanting to disturb them while doing their homework. Although it was not typical, there were several nights that Jacob would have to return to the shop to make a deadline, so they were not concerned.

Of course, the hope was that Jacob would be found quickly and would be unharmed. No one could bring themselves to imagine it could be anything else.

The following morning, Rachel sent the kids off to school before Ariel came over to stay with her. Heschel, David, and Anthony returned to their respective shops just in case someone tried to contact them. Driving aimlessly around the state would do no one any good. They were looking for a needle in a haystack. The best bet would be to find some kind of clue at the cabin in Caribou as what Josef had been planning. Anthony's associates were at the cabin scouring every inch of it for some sign of what Josef had planned.

"Ariel, I am going out of my mind with fear," Rachel said. "How could Jacob have kept this secret from me for so long? I have always loved him with all my heart, and now this murdering pedophile has infiltrated our lives, and God only knows what he will do to my Jacob. The men must find them. Jacob is a quiet, peaceful man who would never harm a soul. This Josef had to have awakened a demon in him that fostered revenge. He apparently would never get over the shame and hurt once he realized that this man was within arm's reach.

"Even so, he wouldn't allow bodily harm to come to him. He found a way to punish him without hurting a hair on his head. Josef has no one to blame but himself for the situation he put himself in."

Of course, men like Josef never take accountability for anything they do. To think otherwise would be naive.

Back in Stockbridge, Jacob was now awake. Josef had put him out with ether, and other than a pounding headache, Jacob was once again awake and aware. He found himself tied at the ankles and chained to a heavy metal spike in the floor.

"Tell me, Josef, what do you plan to do with me? If your plan is to kill me, then just do it already and get it over with."

"Oh no, Jacob. That would be too easy. After all, you sent me to exile and shut me off from the world. Do you really think I would let you off easier? I have plans for us, and when we're through, I have plans for your family."

This thought made Jacob retch inside. He may not have had an easy beginning to his life, and it appeared that he wasn't going to have an easy ending either, but to think of even a hair of his children's lives being hurt was unimaginable. Rachel!

Oh my god.

It suddenly occurred to Jacob that Rachel must be frantic by now. He knew that Heschel, David, and Anthony would cover for him, but now it's been over twenty-four hours, and they must be consumed with fear.

What, he asked himself, *are they telling the children? More importantly, what have they told Rachel? What must Rachel be thinking?*

"So tell me, Josef, what do you intend to do with me? Can you even tell me where we are?"

"You will know soon enough, Jacob. In the meantime, to show you that I am not completely mad, I will allow you to use the bathroom and freshen up. Don't even try to run because there is no place to run to and there is no one to hear you. Also, there are bears and fisher cats out there. Maybe even a mountain lion. Trust me, that is not how you want to die.

"I will untie you and let you use the bathroom, but remember, I can put you out in less than a minute. You will notice that there is no door to the bathroom either. I'm sure you're not a modest man."

With that being said, Josef let out a boisterous howl as though he were howling at the moon. "Yes, I think I am enjoying this."

The first thing Jacob noticed as he entered the bathroom was that there was a window, but it had been bordered up. There was a shower stall, but no curtain. Any kind of privacy was out of the question.

He knew it was getting dark outside, and whatever was going to happen was probably not going to happen tonight. It did feel good though to wash his face and relieve himself.

As he entered the living room, he could smell the fish cooking on the stove. Jacob thought to himself, *I hope his plans are not to starve me to death as he makes me watch him fill his stomach.*

"Come, sit down at the table. I have poured you a nice glass of wine to have with dinner."

Astonishing, Jacob thought. *Here is this madman who has kidnapped me, made me drive us to God knows where, and then puts me out with ether, offering me a glass of wine. I suppose he's not planning to kill me by starvation after all. Okay, I'll sit at your table and I will drink your wine, but where is this hospitality coming from?*

Jacob's mind was whirling. *What does this madman want to do with me?*

At this point, Jacob's mind was going in and out of his reality, of his surroundings.

"Oh my god, Josef, what have you done to me?"

"Not to worry, Jacob, you'll be fine. Well, maybe in a week or two, but you'll be fine. Most importantly, I'll be even better."

Chapter 63

So Many Questions

The following day, Jacob had now been gone for almost forty-eight hours. The children were beginning to get suspicious. Rachel's story, for the most part, was that he ended up on a business trip and would be home in about a week. It was difficult trying to make someone believe something one knew was a fallacy.

On the third day, Steven approached Rachel. "Mom, I am not stupid. What is going on with Dad, and where is he?"

"Steven, you are my oldest, and I cannot lie to you, but the other children are not to know. Promise me."

"I am here for you in whatever capacity you need me to be, but please, do not ever shut me out again. I am the oldest of the children, and therefore, I hold the responsibility of this family. Now tell me what is really going on."

That being said, Rachel poured her heart out to Steven. He was no longer a child and was quite capable of hearing the truth. He probably would handle it better than she would anyhow.

"Mom, I find this incredulous." Tears began to stream down Steven's face. The thought of this gentleman, who wouldn't hurt a fly, was now being victimized by his old nemesis. "What can I do to help?"

"Steven, we have to make up a believable story for Ben and Sarah. They will never understand the true concept of what has taken place. For that matter, even I don't understand it. Steven, I would like the children to think that Dad is away on a business trip that is taking longer than expected. My hope is that Anthony's associates will find him before any harm has come to him. I cannot show my real feelings, or I will crumble and not be able to get up. This is so surreal. They have to find him quickly. For now, this is like looking for a needle in a haystack."

"Mom, I am here for you and will do whatever you need me to. As much as I am hurting inside, it is my anger that is keeping me going."

Chapter 64

Back at Stockbridge

As soon as Jacob had taken a drink of wine from Josef, he began to feel woozy.

How? he thought. *How could I not suspect that he would drug me?*

As Jacob looked at Josef, Josef's image began to look blurry, and he began to sway from side to side. There was now no denying it, he definitely had been drugged.

As Jacob fell to his side, he was able to get out a few words. "What are you going to do to my family?"

Little else was remembered from that moment on. As Jacob's head hit the floor, a sharp pain ran across the back of his scalp as he sprawled on the ground. His last thoughts were those of Rachel and the children.

"Ah, my landsman, now you shall get a taste of your own medicine. How will you feel when all that is familiar to you is torn away and there is no one to turn to and no one to find you? Yes, you will die up here a lonely, empty shell of a man, and by the time anyone finds you, they will find an empty shell of skin and bone. That is, of course, unless the animals get to you first."

Josef finished off the bottle of wine and ate his dinner like a glutton, all the time getting great satisfaction over the plans that were going over and over in his head.

Only a genius could pull this off, he thought to himself.

His intention was to keep Jacob imagining only the worst scenario until it was the actual time to make his move. He had nothing left to go home to and nothing else to live for anyhow. Exacting revenge on Jacob was his only interest in life. What a juxtaposition. The hunted has hunted the hunter. The grin on his face was almost clownlike evil.

By day 6, Josef had given Jacob only bare rations. He wasn't ready for him to die yet. Watching him suffer gave him so much satisfaction. He allowed him bathroom breaks twice a day, but the rest of the time, he was chained and shackled.

Jacob was a tough man. His resolve was beginning to weaken, but for the most part, he was able to stay strong and not show Josef how fearful he really was. Mostly, his fear was directed to Rachel and his children. His mind managed to stay strong, at least for the time being, by conjuring up plans of escape. There were times that Josef would leave the cabin to go who knows where, but Jacob never knew when he would return.

Try as he might, he could not loosen the chains that bound him, although he thought he may have made some headway with a floorboard. He knew he was gradually going to get weak from lack of nourishment and would stash any food he did not finish under his blanket. He had every nook and cranny of the cabin memorized in case he ever had the opportunity to escape. He was a resourceful man. He never thought that dying here was going to be an option.

Josef made sure that he either drugged Jacob or anesthetized him with ether anytime he was going to be gone for any length of time. This was why on day 8 of Jacob's captivity, he woke up in total darkness with no idea how long Josef had been gone. The cabin was silent and empty. Certainly, by now, Josef would have returned to allow Jacob his bathroom break. It seemed as though hours passed, and still no sighting of Josef.

By now, Jacob was sitting in his own excrement and getting very thirsty. There was no water or food within reach.

Perhaps, this was Josef's plan all along. He just wants me to wither away in this desolate place with no food, no water, no anything. Well, if it takes every last breath in my body, he will not have his way.

The stake he was chained to was solidly planted in the floor, down to the ground beneath.

I may not be Houdini, but there must be a way to release myself from here.

Jacob's feet were tied together at the ankles and the knees.

I will start with my ankles. If I can get my legs free, then I should be able to stand up and work on freeing my wrists.

Suddenly, the adrenaline came rushing into his body, and with all his might, he began to pull on the ties around his ankles. At first, they wouldn't budge an inch, but Jacob was persistent and pulled and stretched and pulled and stretched. It seemed like hours had gone by, but he finally got some give going in the ties.

I'll be damned, you bastard, if I'm going to die here after all I've been through.

Jacob could not believe that the sun was starting to rise with still no sign of Josef. He would take short breaks, build up his strength, and pull and stretch some more. Finally, he felt a short give around his ankle. Adrenaline was now reaching an all-time high as his ankle gave way. His feet were finally free.

Freeing his knees seemed to be a bit easier. It still took a couple of hours, but at last, Jacob could stand.

With all his weight, he thrust his body around the stake, first one way, then the other. The pain was excruciating, but he couldn't stop now. The stake went from under the floorboards up through the roof. Still, he knew that if he kept up this force, it would ultimately have to give, even if it took some of the roof with it.

By late morning, Josef still had not returned. Jacob knew that if he ever returned before he got free, it would be his last chance at freedom. By now, he was exhausted. He was thirsty, he was hungry, and he needed a rest, but to stop now may mean the end of him.

With that in mind, he mustered up all the energy a human possibly could and gave one final thrust around this metal stake as a beam began to loosen from the ceiling. With all his might, Jacob pulled one last time on this huge stake as a beam came crashing from the ceiling. Jacob didn't even care if it fell on him. He just knew he had to get away even if it killed him.

Fortunately, he was safe. The beam released the stake so that Jacob could shimmy his wrists down to the shorter end. The cabin was a disaster, but he was free.

Dragging his chains, he crawled over to a sink and took care of his thirst. Getting rid of the chains would require time and tools, which he had neither. His legs and ankles were sore and swollen, but this did nothing to dampen his spirit. He must get to a phone to let Rachel and Heschel know he's going to be okay.

He still had no idea where Josef had gone. Josef could be just outside in the woods, watching, waiting. With that thought in mind, Jacob armed himself with the sharpest kitchen knife he could find. Rummaging through a closet, he grabbed a pair of shoes and a jacket. He still had no idea of where he was or how long he had been gone.

Jacob burst through the door. By now, it was nearing twilight, and he had to get his bearings before the sun went down. He scoured the area for a full 360 degrees but saw no sign of life. He watched the sun go down in the west, so he ventured in the opposite direction. No matter what, he knew he had to travel east. Eventually, he hoped to find some sign of life. All he had on his mind at this point was letting his family know he was all right.

Jacob knew that the woods could be a dangerous place in the dark, so he made himself alert to all sounds and signs. It could be an animal, or worse, it could be Josef. No matter, he just kept walking.

Suddenly, a narrow river came into his view. The sound of the rushing water was music to his ears. He came upon the river, filled his thirst, and decided to just follow the river downstream. It may have been hours later, or just felt like it, but suddenly, a light shone in the distance. By now, Jacob was close to collapsing, but nothing could break his stride to get to that light.

It was not a house but a campsite. Could it be Josef?

No matter, he thought.

He had to come out of the darkness and present himself. When he approached the campsite, which was inhabited by two rugged hunters, he collapsed facedown on the ground.

At first, the men looked on in disbelief. Here was this totally disheveled man who looked as if he hadn't eaten in days. His clothes were torn and tattered, and he was barely audible.

They quickly took him into their tent, washed him, and covered him with blankets. His arms and legs were swollen and bruised. His story would have to wait.

For the next two hours, Jacob went in and out from consciousness as these two kind men tended to him. He had finally reached his breaking point and allowed himself to sleep.

By the next morning, Jacob was fully awake when one of the men brought him in a hot cup of coffee. He knew he owed them a complete explanation, but first, he had to get to a telephone.

"Please," he admonished. "I must get to a phone and will then tell you everything. I have been kidnapped but managed to get away. I have to let my family know I am all right."

The taller of the men, whose name was Charlie, asked if he should notify the police.

"No, no. Please do not call the authorities. At least not until I know what has become of my captor. If you could drive me to a telephone, I will let my family know where I am, and they will come and get me. By the way, where are we?"

When Rachel answered the phone and realized that it was Jacob, she broke down in a floodgate of tears. "Jacob, where are you, are you all right?"

Heschel, who had not left Rachel's side since this all began, grabbed the phone from her and was equally as emotional. "My god, Jacob, I was beginning to think I would never see you again. Please let me know where you are, and I will have Anthony's men come and get you."

"Heschel, I have no idea where I am, but I will put someone on the phone who can instruct you. First, tell me, have you heard from Josef?"

As Charlie gave Heschel the directions to where they were, Charlie's friend, Ted, picked up some food from the local grocery and brought it back to the campsite. It would be at least two hours before anyone got there to pick up Jacob. The men sat around the fire, wrapped in blankets, eating eggs, bacon, and bread. Jacob was famished.

Jacob felt that he owed these men the partial truth about his life and how he got here, so he poured his heart out to these two compassionate men. He couldn't let out the real reason he so hated Josef, but he described being accosted in Poland and the events that followed.

Ted and Charlie were astounded. Jacob was forever grateful. He felt safe for the first time in a very long time.

Although both men were so much taller than Jacob, they let him wash up in the river and gave him some clean clothes to put on. Jacob was beginning to feel human once again. Still, where was Josef?

Chapter 65

Going Home

By late afternoon, the men drove into town and waited for Anthony and his men to pick up Jacob. As the car came around the corner, a wall of tears, mostly of relief, came pouring down Jacob's face.

Anthony was first out of the car and threw his arms around his old friend and partner. All Charlie and Ted could do at this point was watch and feel overcome with pride that they had helped this man reunite with his family.

David came rushing over next and practically threw Jacob down with the force of his bear hug. Heschel decided to stay behind and be with Rachel. They still had much to work out on how they were going to explain things to Ben and Sarah.

Jacob turned to Charlie and Ted and promised to get in touch with them at a later date. He had much to be thankful to them for. They exchanged information and said their goodbyes. Jacob made them promise to not discuss any of this with anyone yet.

All that being said, Jacob got into the car with Anthony and David and headed for home. The discussion on the way home centered entirely on Josef and where he might be or if he was still a danger to anyone. Jacob was so relieved to be going home, but the dark shadow of Josef still hung over his head.

Anthony reassured him that now they knew the vicinity of where Jacob was being held, his men would go up to the cabin and scour the woods for any sign of Josef or of Jacob's car. It was possible that Josef had just taken off in it and gone God knows where. By now, Jacob was certain that Josef was aware that he had escaped. He proved to be a lethal force to be reckoned with, and Jacob would always be looking over his shoulder until he knew where Josef was.

The two-plus hours it took to get home made this the longest ride Jacob had ever had. He couldn't wait to get home to Rachel and the kids. As they approached the street, he did all he could do to stop from jumping out of the car. Apparently, Rachel felt the same way. As soon as she saw the car approaching, she ran up to it and grabbed the handle of the door. Whether or not she dragged Jacob out or he jumped out of the car was unclear as they were once again in each other's arms. It was only a little more than a day ago that this seemed an impossible likelihood.

"Oh, Rachel, I will never, ever leave you again. No matter what the circumstance, I will never allow this to happen again."

Jacob had been versed on the story that the younger children had been told and tried to play into it. His appearance, however, told a different story.

Ben, not much younger than Steven, was the first to admonish his mother for her excuses. "Dad, what has happened to you? You look awful. Do not tell me you have been on a business trip."

With that, Sarah began to cry and literally climb onto Jacob. "Papa, where have you been? You look messy and unwell."

Jacob could no longer hold the whole truth from these children whom he loved so much. Small white lies would be okay, so he told them the story about meeting a perspective customer who just wanted his car and made him drive for miles into the western mountains, where he abandoned him and stole his car. He told the story of meeting campers who saved him, and that was that. They would never understand the whole truth, nor did he want to share it with them. Steven was another story.

After a hot shower, a good meal, and lots of hugs and kisses, the children went to bed. Steven stayed behind, and he and Jacob discussed the real truth about what had been going on. Steven was now an adult, and Jacob could confide in him.

"Papa, I have been so worried about you. Mama told me everything, and my heart is fractured over concern for you. You are an amazing man, and I will be here for you in whatever capacity you need me to be. We will find this horrible creature, and I will be your protectorate until he is no longer a threat to any of us. I love you so much and am so happy to have you home."

With this said, Jacob realized the riches of his life. Not even a Josef could possibly take this away from him.

"Steven, I love and respect you, but *I* will always be your protectorate. It is the way it is. Until I die, it is me who must protect my family. Now please go to bed, and be assured that nothing like this will ever happen again."

Feeling blessed to be loved by his wife and children, brothers, and friends, Jacob slept soundly in Rachel's arms that night. Tomorrow would take care of itself.

Epilogue

The following day, Anthony's men scoured the woods near the cabin. The cabin itself did not seem to have been occupied since Jacob's escape. The roof had been caved in, but there was no sign of recent life.

The men went deep into the woods looking for any sight or reference to Josef. They found nothing. On the second day, they got sight of Jacob's car. It was abandoned. The keys were in the ignition but otherwise seemed to be out of place in an off-the-road area.

The men spread out and eventually came to an area with the distinct smell of decay. As they ventured farther into the woods, the odor became more pronounced.

Maggots and droppings were surrounding what appeared to be the carcass of an animal. On further inspection, they realized the animal was human. The tattered and worn clothes contained a wallet with identification. Lying nearby was a shovel and a partially dug grave. Apparently, Josef had met up with an angry bear or mountain lion that showed him the meaning of karma.

Acknowledgement

I would like to thank my fourth-grade teacher, Mr. Willett, who inspired a nine-year-old to never stop writing. The assignment was to write a poem about Spring. He was so impressed that he made me recite it to the entire school. His inspirational comment has stayed with me my entire life.

He sat me down, looked me in the eye and told me that I would someday be a great writer. Don't ever stop writing.

It may have taken me many decades to write this book, but I never did stop writing. Teachers are a precious gift who can inspire, no matter how young you may be. Thank you again, Mr. Willett.

Spring:
The snow is falling
The trees are bare
but Spring is coming very near

The flowers will bloom
The trees have leaves
Because the sun will glare with ease

The pond will turn to water
Our skates we'll put away
Because Spring is coming closer
Each and every day

About the Author

Shirley B. Novack is a first-generation daughter of Polish and Russian immigrants. She originally graduated from Fisher College in Boston with a degree in laboratory science, but after marrying and having three children, she went back to school and graduated from Newbury College with a degree in interior design. She has had a successful interior design practice since 1985, but her passion for writing was never far from the surface.

This book is loosely based on the life of her father, a Russian immigrant, who was never a wealthy or successful businessman but taught her the importance of being humble and dignified.

She has always wanted to write this story, even though much of it is fictional, but it is an homage to her father and became a labor of love.

Shirley resides in Framingham, Massachusetts, with her husband, Barry, and their precious Havanese, Stevie Nicks.

CPSIA information can be obtained
at www.ICGtesting.com
Printed in the USA
BVHW092044050722
641302BV00015B/355